LEAVING LINCOLNSHIRE

- IN CHAINS

David J. Porter

Illustrated by Jennifer Evans

2010

Published by
Burning Ambition Publications
19 Hillcroft Crescent
London W5 2SG
ISBN 978-0-9559644-1-1

By the same author

From Almondsbury to Aylmer: The Pearce Letters
Burning Ambition Publications, 2008
ISBN 978-0-9559644-0-4

LEAVING LINCOLNSHIRE

- IN CHAINS

FOREWORD

William Tennant was a forerunner of mine as both the Parish Priest of Witham on the Hill and Edenham. His parishes are the setting for my daily ministry, and the landscape that David Porter describes is integral to my life. In many respects the story of John Porter opens up many continuities - not least the unfolding of the story of the Porter family and their dispersion across the British Empire. In other ways it is a reminder that 'the past is a foreign country'. David Porter has also reconstructed for the reader, in convincing detail, the tragic events that precipitated the break up of his forebear's family. This focus on the particular provides vivid illumination to some of the great universal themes of human experience - the use of power, the nature of justice, the indomitable will to survive. This book provides the reader with plenty to stimulate both the heart and the mind.

David's achievement in this account is to set the story of one man and his family in the political, economic and religious context of the time with both fairness and accuracy. I know from my conversations with David that he has taken extraordinary care to 'get things right'; because of this attention to detail it is a very fair and accurate account. The most enjoyable aspect of this book for me has been David's ability to resurrect the characters involved to the extent that I would not be surprised to meet them some time in Lound or Witham on the Hill or walking the footpath to Castle Bytham. I am sure every reader will be grateful to David for re-awakening both William Tennant and John Porter and their neighbours and reminding us that their story is our story too.

Canon Andrew Hawes
Vicar of Edenham with Witham on the Hill
and Swinstead in the Diocese of Lincoln

CONTENTS

LIST OF FIGURES

PREFACE

Leaving Lincolnshire - In Chains is a case study in migration within and from England and is based on the experiences of the author's family. These migrations were not all voluntary. The story begins with a forced migration: the exile of the head of one branch of the family to Australia in 1836. The difficulties and disruption this created for those left behind prompted a series of additional migrations by other family members. The circumstances that caused each to choose to relocate, whether within England or thousands of miles away, were different. The book examines the reasons for migration, where and when each migrant chose to go, and how they got there.

Migrations have always been part of the human story. From the beginning of mankind they have occurred all round the world in a variety of forms, voluntary or forced. Britain has received waves of immigrants down the centuries and has encouraged, sponsored and supported the migrations of many of its citizens. The cases covered in this book are primarily concerned with nineteenth-century British emigration, but examples from other centuries are given in chapter 7.

The Porter family had been residents of the one parish, Witham on the Hill in south-west Lincolnshire, for over a century, but they scattered following the trial, conviction and transportation of the first member of the family to migrate more than a few miles from his place of birth. The story begins with the slaughtering of a single sheep and the repercussions from that event. Now, a century and three-quarters later, we can look at the relative merits of 'moving on' or 'staying put', as well as the effects of migration on those left behind.

During the eighteenth century the Porters appear to have been somewhat better off than most of their neighbours, but circumstances can change quickly. In the early nineteenth century life in England for agricultural labourers took a decided turn for the worse. Serious

Figure 0.1 Emigrant Depot, Birkenhead
Image based on one in *Illustrated London News,* 10 July 1852

recession, the economic effects of prolonged warfare, the agricultural revolution and legislation that radically changed British farming, and institutional corruption all contributed to the causes of migration. Pre-Victorian England faced serious problems.

This book would not exist if it were not for the records and research conducted by my mother, Helen Porter, from the 1940s onwards. In addition, a number of descendants of the Porter family in Canada have provided me with photographs and other information in more recent years. Research assistance in England has been received from Peter Crane, Pam Scott, Hazel Wenham, Janice O'Brien, Chris and Sheila Collins, the Revd Andrew Hawes, Canon of Lincoln Cathedral and vicar of Witham on the Hill, and many other friends.

Many hours have been spent in libraries and archives in the course of preparing this book. My thanks are due to helpful staff at the Lincolnshire Archives and the Lincoln City Library, the National Archives, the Guildhall Library, Greenwich Heritage Centre and Lloyds Registry of Shipping in London. The Mitchell Library, State Library of New South Wales, has helped to inform the Australian content. The Canadian research was conducted primarily in the Ontario Archives, Elgin County Archives and the St Thomas City Library with assistance from Bruce Johnson of the Elgin County Branch of the Ontario Genealogy Society.

All the artwork, illustrations, maps and cover design have been produced by Jenny Evans. Credits for photographs are due to Andrew Jenkins, George Porter, Joe and Kim Cornelissen, Jim Porter, Marjorie Bossuyt, Joan Le Boeuf, and my wife Sandy. This book has been edited by Faith Bowers with significant input from her husband Brian and I am extremely grateful to them both for their professional advice and assistance.

Leaving Lincolnshire - In Chains is dedicated to my grandchildren, Molly, Lucy and Cohen, because I believe that one day they will be curious about their origins.

David Porter
London, England
July 2010

Figure 0.2 Map of England and Wales showing Lincolnshire
Lincoln, the county town, is 140 miles north of London

CHAPTER 1

JUST ANOTHER BAPTISM

In the autumn of 1836, the Reverend William Tennant performed one of the several hundred baptisms he administered during his career. But this one was different. The harvest was in full swing so agricultural labourers who were able to find employment for this season were busy in the fields that Monday in late September.

In the village of Castle Bytham, a woman brings her child to the parish church to be baptised. Almost everyone is busy at work and life appears normal. The church is a solid old stone building. When the woman knocks at the door, the curate opens it and the woman and her three-year-old child enter. No-one appears happy.

Figure 1.1 Exterior of St James' Church, Castle Bytham

The curate leads the mother and her child to the baptismal font, while on a table nearby, the Baptismal Register for this parish awaits today's new entry. The curate knows every person and family in his small rural parish. The Baptismal Register confirms that this curate has conducted almost all of the baptisms, marriages and burials since his arrival in the parish a decade earlier, most recently the christening of one of his own sons. He is a very busy person with responsibilities extending to other neighbouring parishes, so today's baptism must be brief. He needs to attend to other important business.

Figure 1.2 Interior of Castle Bytham Church before renovations in 1900
The text on the arch is taken from Psalm 97, 'The Lord is King, the earth be glad thereof. Yea, the multitude of the isles may be glad thereof'.

But something is odd. The child's father is not present and the mother looks downcast as she presents her child to the curate. There is no eye contact between mother and curate. The curate is solemn as he dips his hand into the holy water, then asks the mother, 'What do you name this child?' She answers quietly, 'Frederick'. Frederick has three older brothers, but none of them are present. The two older boys are busy labouring in the fields and her seven-year-old is at home, too ill to attend. There were few to witness the event.

Figure 1.3 Curate, mother and child at baptismal font

The curate mutters some inaudible words about the child's soul, touches Frederick's forehead with his wet fingers and promptly hands him back. The ceremony over, the curate finishes his task by recording Frederick's baptism in the Register.

Baptisms are intended to be uplifting celebrations, but not this one. On this September day the adults present knew what was wrong and so did everyone else in the village of Castle Bytham. Frederick's father had been charged with sheep stealing and was in prison awaiting trial. The slaughtered sheep was not just any sheep but one belonging to the curate. As he and the woman holding her newly baptised child turn and walk in opposite directions they both know that, if convicted, the sentence for sheep stealing would be harsh: life imprisonment, transportation to a penal colony far from home or, perhaps, even death.

Everyone in Castle Bytham knows that the slaughtered sheep belonged to the curate, and he is angry, very angry, and vigorously pressing a serious criminal charge against his only suspect, the woman's husband. The sheep had a market value of just one pound. So why did the Revd William Tennant, curate of Castle Bytham, pursue this case at all?

The case studies that follow were triggered by the outcome of the trial which was about to take place in South Lincolnshire. Frederick's father, John Porter, was convicted and sentenced to life imprisonment and transportation to His Majesty's Penal Colony in New South Wales. This forced migration of John Porter is examined in detail, based on the records of his imprisonment in England, his voyage to Australia, and his fate until he was eventually granted his Ticket of Leave by the Governor of NSW, ten years after his arrival there.

The forced migration of the head of the family requires the remaining members of the family to adapt quickly. The cases of John's wife and his four young sons are also examined. Three of his sons survived to reach adulthood and each of their separate migrations to Canada are also included. All of John Porter's siblings promptly pulled up sticks, leaving their rural environment for the security provided by the nearest market town.

Page 81						

BAPTISMS solemnized in the Parish of *Castle Bytham*
in the County of *Lincoln* — in the Year 1836

When Baptized.	Child's Christian Name.	Parents Name.		Abode.	Quality, Trade, or Profession.	By whom the Ceremony was performed.
		Christian.	Surname.			
1836 May 9 No. 641.	Charles Son of	Joseph and Elizabeth	Coy	Castle Bytham	Butcher and Farmer	William Tennant Curate
May 14th No. 642.	Stephen Son of	James and Elizabeth	Kettle	Counthorpe	Labourer	William Tennant Curate
May 23d No. 643	William Henry Son of	Robert and Catherine	Glenn	Castle Bytham	Labourer	William Tennant Curate
May 29th No. 644	Frank Son of	Edward and Susannah	Harris	Castle Bytham	Labourer	William Tennant Curate
July 2nd No. 645.	Samuel Son of	William and Rebecca	Palmer	Castle Bytham	Farmer	William Tennant Curate
July 4th No. 646.	Harriet Daughter of	Hugh and Catherine	Stanham	Castle Bytham	Farmer	William Tennant Curate
July 4th No. 647.	Alfred Son of	William and Katherine	Tennant	Castle Bytham	Clerk in Orders	William Tennant Curate
Sept 26th No. 648	Fredrick Son of	John and Ann	Porter	Counthorpe	Labourer	William Tennant Curate

**Figure 1.4 Page from the Castle Bytham Baptismal Register
recording the baptism of Frederick Porter**

John's parents were too elderly to migrate and both died shortly after their son's conviction and sentence. John's wife was the only surviving member of the family who did not migrate and her case is also included.

The cases of two of John Porter's sons, John his eldest and Frederick his youngest, at first seem similar; but they differ in important ways. Young John went to Canada by himself in 1852, while Frederick migrated within England to find work in the cotton mills in the North. It turned into a dreadful experience and he too migrated to Canada three decades after his elder brother.

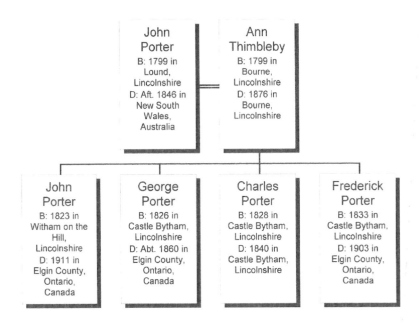

Figure 1.5 Family of John Porter and Ann Thimbleby

A TALE OF TWO PARISHES

The initial setting for this story is found in rural villages of South Lincolnshire. In the early nineteenth century, Lincolnshire was England's second largest county by area, but ranked only fifth or sixth by population. The county of Lincolnshire was described as:

> bounded on the north by the river Humber, which separates it from Yorkshire; on the east by the German Ocean; on the south by Cambridgeshire and Northamptonshire; and on the west by the counties of Rutland, Leicester, Nottingham and York: its form is an irregular oblong; in length from north to south, it is 77 miles; in breadth, about 48.
>
> Pigot & Co., *National and Commercial Directory*, 1828-9

From ancient times, Lincolnshire has been divided into three subparts: Lindsey and Holland in the north and Kesteven in the south. Our story begins in two relatively small parishes in Kesteven, Castle Bytham and Witham on the Hill. The map at Fig. 1.6 shows these and some of the neighbouring parishes relevant to this book.

Kesteven was primarily a rural area, heavily reliant upon agriculture. Pigot says the agricultural produce of the county was principally 'sheep, meat cattle, horses and corn. The sheep are large, clothed with long thick wool, peculiarly serviceable for the worsted and coarse woollen manufacturers, of which great quantities are annually sent into Yorkshire and other counties.' There was very little local manufacturing or industry, but with Britain's rapidly increasing population, there was growing demand from beyond Lincolnshire for food and other agricultural products.

The times were difficult. The French Revolution (1789) had eliminated royalty and aristocracy there. The wealth-owning classes in Britain had watched the French and American Revolutions create republics based upon the principle of equality among all citizens and they feared a similar revolution in Britain. The ruling class was well aware of rising tensions throughout the country. They were ready to use the full force of their power to crush any who challenged their authority.

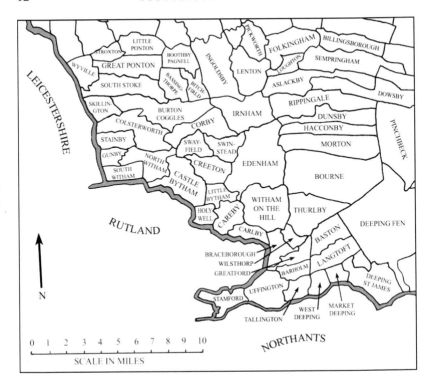

Figure 1.6 Some parishes in South Kesteven

Long years of warfare, with America and Napoleonic France and its allies, had depleted Britain's resources. Peace had swamped the country with men returning from the armed forces and seeking employment. Agriculture itself was seeing sweeping changes. The centuries-old communal system of farming was being replaced with larger units for more efficient production, but this made life harder for those who did not own land. Enclosure Acts ended the medieval strip system which had enabled villagers to grow their own food and much of the common land used for animals was now being lost to them.

Some of the most powerful men in South Lincolnshire were involved in the trial of John Porter, accused of killing a single sheep. These were wealthy, influential, landed gentry. Across the courtroom they would face a barely literate agricultural labourer.

Castle Bytham and Witham on the Hill were four miles apart, separated by the smaller parishes of Little Bytham and Careby. Both lay on relatively high ground, well suited for livestock and crops and enjoyed similar picturesque landscapes. More important, the ownership of land was vested in a few wealthy persons in both parishes. The history of this area can be traced back for hundreds of years and there are references to people and places in both parishes in the Domesday Book (effectively a census taken in 1086). Most of the landowners could trace their lineage back for centuries.

The Parish of Castle Bytham shares a boundary with the County of Rutland and contains a village bearing the same name. Most of the buildings in the village were constructed of stone, with sprawling cottages among its steep streets. Castle Bytham is an ancient place, with only the earthworks remaining from the Castle, which Henry III beseiged in 1221 and which was burned later during the Wars of the Roses (1455-1485). In addition to the village of Castle Bytham, the parish contained two hamlets, Counthorpe and Holywell. In the early nineteenth century, Castle Bytham was described as

> a considerable village, picturesquely seated on a bold eminence between two rivulets, 5 miles S. of Corby and 9 miles N.N.W. of Stamford, increased its population from 372 souls in 1801, to 671 in 1841 and has in its township 4007 A[cres]. of land. Its parish includes also the townships of Counthorpe and Holywell cum Aunby. Here was an ancient castle, or fortified mansion, which belonged to Lord Hussey, in the reign of Henry VII ... a great part of the soil belongs to Sir G. Heathcote, G. A. F. Heathcote, Esq., the Rev. William Tennant, the Dean and Chapter of Lincoln, and a few smaller owners.
>
> *White's History, Gazetteer & Directory*, 1842

Sir Gilbert Heathcote was a Baronet and a Member of Parliament for Lincolnshire 1796-1806. He then represented the County of Rutland in Parliament 1812-1841. On his death in 1851, he was succeeded in the baronetcy by his son, also named Gilbert. Sir Gilbert, the elder, will appear as one of the two judges at the trial.

White also gives information about the parish church in Castle Bytham, which belonged to the Church of England's diocese of Lincoln:

> The Church (St. James) is a neat fabric, with a tower and three bells. The living is...in the incumbency of the Rev. Charles Althorpe Wheelwright, and alternative patronage of the Bishop and Dean and Chapter of Lincoln. The latter are appropriations of the rectory, of which the Rev. William Tennant is lessee.

Castle Bytham's two hamlets, Holywell and Counthorpe, were both small but very different in character. Holywell, located two miles south of the village of Castle Bytham, contained 98 inhabitants; a picturesque ivy-covered stone church and Holywell Hall. The Lord of the Manor, Lieutenant General Thomas Birch Reynardson, lived in Holywell Hall and, according to White, owned the soil, meaning all 2,350 acres of fertile and well-wooded land. Thomas Birch had assumed the additional surname and arms of Reynardson on the death of his father-in-law. Acting in his role as magistrate, Thomas Birch Reynardson would issue the indictment that would direct that the defendant be arrested and brought to trial.

At the other extreme, Counthorpe, the hamlet two miles north of the village of Castle Bytham, and again mentioned in the Domesday Book, covered an area of 1,129 acres but contained no church or stately home. Its 85 inhabitants lived in six dwellings in the hamlet and on a further six scattered farms. Few, if any, of the inhabitants of Counthorpe owned any land. The defendant and his family merely rented one of the houses in Counthorpe.

Almost every dwelling in the hamlet of Counthorpe was demolished in the 1840s when a new railway carved its way through the parish. There are a few later buildings, but the only pre-railway dwellings that remain in Counthorpe today are the scattered farm houses. A few years before the railway destroyed this tiny hamlet, the heart was torn from one of the original households by the outcome of a trial.

CHAPTER 2

ENGLAND, A GREEN AND PLEASANT LAND?

At the start of this story the Porters were a family settled in the countryside of South Lincolnshire. For many years they appear to have made a decent living as farm workers but by the 1830s times were getting harder.

The main subject of this book is migration: why members of the family moved within or left England, where they went and how they got there. To understand this, some understanding of the state of British society in the 1830s is needed.

COST OF PROLONGED WARFARE

In 1836 Britain was a nation in decline, financially weakened and made weary by wars. Seventy years earlier, Britain had become a world superpower. The Seven Years' War (1756-1763) had spanned the globe, with Britain at the forefront of battles in Central Europe, North America, the Caribbean, West Africa, India and the Philippines. The American historian, Fred Anderson, notes that 'by the end of the Seven Years' War, Britain had thrown France out of North America and India and laid claim to the islands in the French Caribbean, Havana and Manila. But this moment of seeming imperial triumph held within it the seeds of the American Revolution.' The loss of thirteen colonies following the American Revolution (1775-1783) marked a first step in the disintegration of British power.

In 1812 another war between Britain and the United States began, ending in stalemate just over two years later; Britain was fortunate not to lose this war too. This war, however, reinforced a lesson only partially comprehended after the loss of the American colonies: Britain had an urgent need to populate her remaining colonies in North America with settlers who would remain loyal. The War of 1812 proved that, if settlers could not soon be persuaded or encouraged to go to North America the remaining British colonies in that continent ran a serious risk of being overrun and absorbed into the aggressive, thrusting, new Republic on Canada's southern border, the United States of America.

Britain had not only waged war in North America. In 1815, after nearly two decades of fighting, Britain and her allies finally defeated the French at Waterloo. But even this much celebrated victory over Napoleon created problems, when many thousands of returning soldiers and sailors were discharged to seek work back at home. While the Napoleonic wars continued, Britain's economy performed well, particularly after control of the seas was secured at the Battle of Trafalgar in 1805. But the years after 1815 were fraught with difficulty due both to recession and to structural changes in the economy as machines replaced handcrafts. Prolonged warfare had left Britain virtually bankrupt and the economy was in desperate straits.

The soldiers returned to find a period of serious economic recession and a great many did not succeed in finding work. Migration was one obvious solution to the surplus labour problem and sponsored migration schemes were a neat solution. A number of schemes emerged to encourage former soldiers and others, both individuals and families, and even whole communities to relocate abroad. One of these was known as the Petworth Project and more information on this important regional migration scheme can be found in Chapter 7. The Petworth Project is one example of a sponsored migration scheme, but there were many others, most of which were smaller and less well resourced.

RECESSION

Economic historians tell us that the first prolonged recession the world had ever experienced struck the newly industrialised world shortly after the Napoleonic Wars ended in 1815. A recession is a general slowdown in economic activity over a period of time. Before the industrial revolution, recessions did occur, but they were local and tended to be short-lived. Production, employment, investment spending, people's incomes, and profits all tend to fall during recessions, while unemployment increases.

Those engaged in agriculture were deeply affected. With only relatively modest relief from time to time, the recession in the British agricultural sector persisted until the early 1870s. The severity was partially masked by new employment opportunities created by the building of railroads and in the textile industries of northern England. Much of this new employment involved harsh and sometimes dangerous working conditions, child labour, long working hours and low wages.

In mid nineteenth-century Britain many agricultural labourers left the land and migrated to industrial towns and cities, where working conditions might be dangerous and poorly paid, but at least there was employment to be found. The consequences for a family migrating from rural agrarian England to the cotton mills in the north can be seen later in a heartbreaking saga for the Porter family.

INDUSTRIAL REVOLUTION

In 1750 the textile industry was entirely domestic, with skilled self-employed men and women producing linen and woollen cloth, the produce of farming in the British Isles, in their homes or in villages. Imported cotton first made an appearance in Britain in the 1750s and technical developments, which had begun about the same time, allowed yarn to be spun in factories powered by water. These early factories were relatively small and built mostly in the countryside near fast- flowing streams.

Around the beginning of the nineteenth century steam power began to come into general use and steam-powered looms to appear. As the number and size of mills increased, more and more labour was required, and a major migration of the British workforce commenced. Within three decades there were tens of thousands of people at work as power-loom weavers. By the 1830s the textile industry was dominated by cotton manufacture and the workplace had shifted from homes and villages to large factories or mills.

Figure 2.1 An early industrial mill

The revolution in the textile industry stimulated the growth and development of other industries. Mechanical components needed to be designed, engineered and manufactured, raw materials needed to be sourced, processed and transported. Finished products needed to shipped to customers domestically and internationally. Bigger and better ships and ports were needed. The demand for iron and steel products required smelters and forges which in turn required coal for fuel. Mines and collieries were opened and expanded. Canals were dug to transport coal

Figure 2.2 An industrial mill town

and other products, and from 1825 the great age of railway building was under way.

The railways employed people both during their construction and when they became operational. Many navvies migrated from Ireland to join surplus British agricultural workers seeking employment in railway construction. When completed, the railways helped other industries to expand. For example, market gardening developed briskly once fruit and vegetables could reach mass markets before they were spoiled. The railways also played a major role in making the internal migration of people within Britain possible. Nevertheless, traditional agriculture continued to suffer.

The first industrial revolution the world had witnessed was under way in Britain and massive numbers of people were migrating from the countryside to seek work in the new urban industrial centres.

ENCLOSURE MOVEMENT

Those who chose to remain on the farms and continued to depend on agriculture for their livelihood also experienced substantial change to their employment during the early nineteenth century. The Enclosure Movement that began in the mid eighteenth century was an attempt to make the agricultural industry more productive. For centuries, farming in Britain had been conducted on a communal basis, a method of farming introduced into Britain by the Anglo-Saxon migrants in the seventh and eighth centuries. This system began to change in 1742 with the passing of the first Enclosures Acts.

The Anglo-Saxons lived and worked in tribal groups with farming treated as a means of group survival, not individual profit. This developed into the medieval system where the common people, called villeins, had rights to graze and cultivate strips of land to feed their families, in return for their work for the lord of the manor. The lord of the manor could also call on them when he was required to raise his share of an army. Under a good landowner the common people might live quite well, although they were also open to exploitation and abuse.

Farmers knew from experience that land could not be cultivated year after year without loss of fertility and therefore left fields fallow on a rotational basis one year in three or, in some areas, one year in four. Almost everyone was engaged in agriculture and the whole community benefited or suffered together with the risks and rewards that have always existed in the agricultural industry.

Medieval fields were small and scattered but were shared out among the families in each community on a basis concerned more with fairness than efficiency. It was an open-field system with all farmers holding the right to graze animals on the common lands, once the crops were harvested. The system was designed to guarantee the survival of the whole community but as a result any agricultural surpluses were unlikely to be large. Ploughing in medieval times was done by teams of up to eight oxen, which also meant they needed to share resources and provide labour on a communal basis.

Figure 2.3 Ploughing a strip in medieval times

Over the centuries, the system was modified. As the population increased, pressure to increase the amount of land under cultivation grew and some individuals created new 'enclosed areas' for their own use. As time passed these enclosed, privately owned, parcels of land passed to new owners, many of whom were absentee landlords holding large numbers of individual enclosures.

By the mid eighteenth century as more people moved to live in towns, the market for farm produce increased and there was a pressing need to make agriculture much more efficient. The benefits of enclosing the open fields was seen as sufficiently important for the government to encourage agreement to this among landowners or, failing that, by a specific Act of Parliament for which the principal landowners could apply. Altogether there were over 4,000 individual Acts of Parliament enclosing land across the country. Irrespective of how the Enclosure Movement came into being in any particular area, the result was the same. The strip system of land distribution disappeared when land was enclosed and the common people lost out badly.

A few, often absentee, landlords owned the bulk of the enclosed land and common land began to disappear. Few tenants who had previously farmed their strips of land could afford to purchase land. Some were able to rent fields as tenant farmers, but the majority could only become agricultural labourers. Their sons began to migrate in ever increasing numbers to find work in the towns.

Figure 2.4 The Breadbasket
This pleasant nineteenth-century scene shows the Lord of the Manor with his ladies inspecting the labourers and their families during harvest. In reality, life had become very unpleasant for agricultural workers and their families.

THE AGRICULTURAL REVOLUTION

The agricultural revolution, with its improvements to machinery and farming techniques, helped to create the industrial revolution. Although technological innovation was only slowly accepted in such a long-established and traditional industry, by the 1830s improvements to equipment and machinery had considerably reduced the manpower required. Larger farms were indeed more productive, but required less labour. Labourers' wages were driven down and even those who could find employment had difficulty in making ends meet.

The plight of some agricultural labourers was life-threatening. Faced with the choice between stealing food or starving, the case of George Willets makes unpleasant reading. Willets, a farm labourer and a bachelor from 'the low part of Essex', was transported to Australia on the same ship as John Porter. He developed scurvy and the report written by the ship's doctor states that previously Willets

> generally enjoyed good health except during the winter months, when for want of employment and consequent want of proper sustenance has been very weak and emaciated, has for some of the late winters been for months unemployed, could not get work, lived very poorly indeed, *he says* nearly starved at times which induced him to steal a sheep for which he has been transported for life. He is now remarkably thin ...

In addition to treatment for scurvy, which included medicines, barley water with lime juice, cleansing and provision of flannel underwear, the doctor prescribed a better diet: 'To have as much chocolate night and morning as he can use with a double allowance of Bread, ½ lb of preserved meat for dinner, and ½ pint of Wine in the day'. Willets somehow managed to survive his long journey to Australia, and the doctor's report noted 'the worst case that did not terminate fatally'. When they landed at Sydney Willets, although still very poorly, was able with support to walk to the hospital. The poor man had probably enjoyed better care as a prisoner on the convict ship than in his previous life finding what work he could on Essex farms.

The Willets case is just one example of the dire circumstances that some agricultural labourers faced. In the 1830s the male members of the Porter family were all labourers dependent solely on the agricultural industry for their livelihood.

Rapid population growth and agricultural employment

When the 1801 census was taken, officials estimated that the population of England had increased by 77% over the previous 100 years. The following table shows that during the next 100 years, the population increased by 367% (1891 27.2m, 1901 30.5m).

POPULATION GROWTH AND AGRICULTURAL EMPLOYMENT

Year	1801	1811	1821	1831	1841	1851	1861	1871	1881
Total	8.3	9.5	11.2	13.0	14.9	16.8	18.8	21.3	24.4
%	35.9	33.0	28.4	24.6	22.2	21.7	18.7	15.1	12.6

Total population of England in millions
with percentage of the labour force employed in agriculture
Source for population totals: UK Census Records; Source for agricultural labour: Phyllis Deane and A.W. Cole, *British Economic Growth 1688-1959* (Cambridge, 1962)

This table shows that the proportion of the workforce employed in agriculture, forestry and fishing declined continually and steeply through the century. Although 'agricultural labourer' was by far the most common male occupation in Britain at the beginning of the nineteenth century, it soon became a 'dead end' occupation, where there was little prospect of promotion or advancement. Most agricultural labourers lacked the capital to purchase or even rent farms of their own so very few could aspire to become farmers. Their career alternatives were primarily to remain an agricultural labourer for the rest of their life or migrate to find employment in an industrial town or port or migrate abroad where land for settlers was advertised at prices they could afford.

In 1830 the average wage of an agricultural worker was nine shillings a week, but by 1834 the rate had fallen to six shillings. The pressure was mounting.

THE SWING RIOTS

In 1830-31 impoverished and landless agricultural labourers in the south and east of England set out to halt further reductions in their wages and put a stop to the introduction of the new threshing machines that threatened their livelihoods. Widespread rioting was targeted at threshing machines, workhouses and tithe barns.

The leader of the movement was known as Captain Swing (who probably never existed) but threatening letters bearing his name were sent to landowners, farmers, magistrates, clergymen and others. A similar uprising directed at industrial abuses had already begun, lead by the fictional King Ludd. The press was soon aware of the 'Swing Letters' and provided wide coverage of both the letters and the disturbances that followed. The first threshing machine was attacked on 28 August 1830 and within two months over 100 more had been destroyed in East Kent. In Lincolnshire there were a few dozen disturbances.

The riots were attributed to the overwhelming poverty and unemployment faced by England's agricultural workforce in the years leading up to 1830. The rioters' anger was directed primarily at landowners and rich tenant farmers who had introduced new and mechanised agricultural machinery while progressively lowering wages.

By December 1830 nearly 2,000 people had been arrested and were awaiting trial for their involvement in the Swing Riots. Eventually nineteen were executed and over 500 were transported to penal colonies abroad.

The Porters, along with their neighbours, would have felt the impact of these changes. It would have been particularly hard for boys and young men seeking to break into the labour market.

Other factors added to the problems of working families. Lacking the ownership of property meant they had little political clout, but they could still suffer the effects of institutional corruption among the ruling classes. Life in pre-Victorian England was not particularly fair and justice was biased in favour of those with power.

INSTITUTIONAL CORRUPTION

Britain's decline in the early nineteenth century was not solely economic. Abuse of power was widespread in important institutions. Parliament, local government, the army and even the Established Church were all in need of reform. The Porter family and others like them had little influence in society. They had no voting rights and were largely at the mercy of the various established institutions and the ruling classes who ran them.

Rotten Boroughs and Electoral Reform

After Waterloo, public meetings began to take place throughout the country demanding more representative government and an end to the Corn Laws which maintained the price of grain and bread at artificially high levels. Agitation continued and in 1820 culminated in the 'Radical War', with calls for a general strike and what turned out to be an abortive workers' uprising. The uprising was brutally suppressed and a few ringleaders were executed.

Fear of revolution troubled many of the better off, although some of the middle class were in sympathy with the radicals in their campaign for reform of both parliament and local government. There were stormy meetings throughout the 1820s over the highly distorted electoral system. The term 'Rotten Borough' was coined as a result of the widely reported press coverage of these meetings. A Rotten Borough was a parliamentary constituency that had very few electors and was under the control or 'in the pocket' of a local landowner. Any borough with less than 1,000 electors could be a rotten borough if the dominant local landowner was able to impose his candidate with minimal opposition. Those arguing for reform cited the extreme case of Old Sarum, which no longer had any resident electors at all, but returned two MPs until 1832. Slowly but surely the reformers gained the upper hand and eventually triumphed when Parliament passed the Reform Act in 1832.

The Reform Act of 1832 introduced wide-ranging changes to the electoral system. According to its preamble, the Act was designed to: 'take effectual Measures for correcting diverse Abuses that have long prevailed in the Choice of Members to serve in the Commons House of Parliament'. Calls for reform had been mooted for years, perennially without success. The 1832 Act granted seats in the House of Commons to large cities that had sprung up during the industrial revolution and took away seats from the rotten boroughs. The Act also increased the number of individuals entitled to vote, enlarging the size of the electorate by over 50 per cent, which meant that one out of six adult males in a population of some 14 million could now vote.

The 1832 attempt at reform did not go far enough to please all. Not until the 1867 Reform Acts were very small boroughs eliminated; not until 1884 were district voting populations made roughly equal and all agricultural workers were enfranchised. That Third Reform Act tripled the electorate. Only in 1918 were all men over twenty-one given a vote, along with women over thirty; this was extended to women over twenty-one in 1928. But the earliest changes were just enough to avoid violent political upheaval becoming uncontrollable after 1832.

Purchase of Army Commissions

Often progression in some fields of endeavour did not depend on merit, but upon a person's ability to purchase privilege. For example, army commissions (officer ranks) in the cavalry and infantry regiments could be purchased from the late seventeenth century until the practice was abolished by the Cardwell Reforms in 1871.

There were several key reasons for the sale of commissions. First, it ensured that the officer class was largely populated by persons having a vested interest in maintaining the status quo, thereby reducing the possibility of army units taking part in a revolution or coup. Second, by maintaining social exclusivity of the officer class, the purchase of commissions ensured that officers had private financial means and were therefore less likely to engage in looting or pillaging or to cheat the soldiers under their command. Third, disgraced officers could be stripped of their commission without reimbursement. Finally, because an officer could sell his commission, it provided honourably retired officers with an immediate source of capital when required.

The official values of commissions varied by regiment, usually in line with the differing levels of social prestige of different regiments. In 1837 for example, the cost of purchasing ranks was as follows:

Official Values of Commissions 1837

Rank	Life Guards	Cavalry	Foot Guards	Infantry	Half Pay Difference
Cornet/ Ensign	£1,260	£840	£1,200	£450	£150
Lieutenant	£1,785	£1,190	£2,050	£700	£365
Captain	£3,500	£3, 225	£4,800	£1,800	£511
Major	£5,350	£4,575	£8,300	£3,200	£949
Lieutenant Colonel	£7,250	£6,175	£9,000	£4,500	£1,314

These prices were not incremental, so to purchase a promotion an officer only had to pay the difference in price between his existing rank and the new one. In theory, a commission could be sold only for its official value, and was to be offered first to the next most senior officer in the same regiment but this rule was frequently abused.

Abuse in the Established Church

A number of historians demonstrate that the Established Church had become corrupt, with positions in the church, like the army, available by purchase. Income tied to those positions often made investment in ecclesiastical positions a lucrative proposition.

Kenneth Hylson-Smith in *The Churches in England from Elizabeth I to Elizabeth II Volume III 1833-1998* (London, 1998) describes the growing perception that existed in the 1830s that the Church of England had become corrupt:

> On many occasions in the seventeenth and eighteenth centuries the cry had gone up that the Church of England was in danger; but at no time since it was established in the sixteenth century was the danger to its status and authority, if not its very existence, greater than in 1833. The 1820s had been a bad decade for the national church. It had always had its critics, but the whole tide of increased radicalism, and the widespread demand for change in various aspects of national life, gave the more extreme detractors a larger and more sympathetic audience than they might have had in any previous age. Radical writers such as Richard Carlile, William Sherwin and the ex-Anglican London clergyman Robert Taylor were severe in their condemnation of the established church, and characterized it as the 'corrupt and bloated lackey of the unreformed system'.

A contemporary writer, John Wade, published the widely read *Black Book: or Corruption Unmasked* (London, 1829) in which he attacked not only the church but the Tory establishment in its widest sense, including the monarchy, the civil list, the aristocracy, the Bank of England and the East India Company. The Tories had been in power almost continuously since the early years of the French Revolution. Initially, Wade sold 14,000 copies, then, as public interest in the stand he was taking proved overwhelming, a further 50,000 copies were printed and sold. The unrest within England had become frightening, but the primary target of Wade's criticism was the Established Church and the abuses and corruption he saw in plural livings, absenteeism and the gross disparities of clergy income compared to the rest of society.

The fierceness of anti-clerical hostility was clearly demonstrated during the Swing Riots of 1830-31 and was intensified by the strong and very public way the Church of England postured against political reform. The climax was reached when the bishops in the House of Lords helped to stop the Reform Bill in its tracks in 1831 by voting twenty-one to two against its passage into law.

Hylson-Smith's observations are echoed by other prominent scholars, including Owen Chadwick in his two-volume work, *The Victorian Church* (1966 and 1970). Chadwick sums up this sad episode in British history with:

> The tide of popular rage poured itself against the House of Lords, the peers, the Tory leadership, and conspicuously upon the bishops.

Britain was a nation in decline in the 1830s and social, political and economic reform was urgently needed.

CHAPTER 3

DOWN ON THE FARM

The previous chapter examined the state of the nation; this one looks at life in the hamlets and villages of the two small parishes in South Lincolnshire in the decades leading up to the 1830s. The Porter family are introduced and also the local curate, William Tennant.

It is not uncommon to find families throughout England with pedigrees that prove that they have lived continuously in the same parish for several centuries. There are, however, relatively few records of ordinary families before the seventeenth century. About 1601 parish records were required in order to comply with the Poor Law, so from then on it becomes possible to learn rather more of the lives of ordinary folk.

Figure 3.1 St Andrew's, Witham on the Hill
The tombstone of John Porter is in the foreground

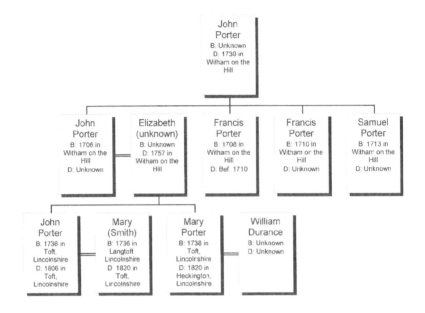

Figure 3.2 The first three generations

The earliest parish records that survive for the Parish of Witham on the Hill begin in 1670 and entries that name the Porter family begin in 1706 when a John Porter is named in the parish baptismal registers as the father of four sons. His eldest, also named John, was baptised in 1706, Francis in 1708, another Francis in 1710 (implying that the first had died in infancy), and Samuel in 1713.

Many of these early parish records are difficult to read and gaps occur where records are missing. There is a burial record for a John Porter in 1739, which we may assume relates to the father of these boys. In all probability his ancestors had lived in or near this village for a long time.

The John Porter baptised in 1706 appears to have had at least two children who survived to adulthood. One was a son also named John, born in 1736. Fortunately, when this John died in 1806 at the age of seventy, he left a Will which named his wife, Mary; a sister also called Mary, who was the widow of William Durance of Heckington, and four of his own children: John, Mary, Ann and Robert.

Since the name John Porter appears in seven consecutive generations in this book, a method of distinguishing one from another is required. Therefore the year of their birth and death will follow their name until no longer necessary in each section. The Porter family finally discovered middle names in 1865. The overall naming system follows, with dates as known:

Generation	Name	Spouse	Locations
First	John Porter (? - 1739)	Not known	Witham on the Hill
Second	John Porter (1706-?)	Possibly Elizabeth	Witham on the Hill
Third	John Porter (1736-1806)	Mary (Smith)	Toft
Fourth	John Porter (1763-1837)	Charlotte Nightingale	Toft, then Lound
Fifth	John Porter (1799-after 1846)	Ann Thimbleby	Lound, Castle Bytham, Australia
Sixth	John Porter (1823-1911)	Rosanna Disher	Lound, Castle Bytham, Canada
Seventh	John George Porter (1865-1956)	Inez Crosby	Canada and USA

Figure 3.3 Seven generations of John Porters

The exact places of abode within the parish of Witham on the Hill for the Porter family during the earliest generations is not known because the records during this period only named the parish, but it is clear from these and other records that the Porter family had lived and worked in this parish without interruption for a very long time. They were neither rich nor poor but appear to have maintained a normal, comfortable existence and lived harmoniously alongside their neighbours throughout the eighteenth century.

We know quite a lot about John Porter (1736-1806). His wife's name was Mary (probably Mary Smith of Langtoft, but this has not been proven). Together they had fourteen children whose baptisms are recorded in the parish records between 1760 and 1780. Nine of these died in infancy and their burials also appear in the parish records. Curiously, for nineteen years the mother's name is entered in the registers as Elizabeth, but when the son Thomas is baptised in 1780, the mother's name is entered in the register as Mary for the first time and, for all the previous entries in both the baptismal and burial records, the name Elizabeth is crossed out and replaced by the name Mary. The most likely explanation relates to a change of vicar: Thomas Foster, the previous vicar left in the 1770s and was replaced by Charles Woolsey Johnson. The Johnson family had lived in the parish for a very long time, knew the Porter family, and probably realised that the earlier entries were incorrect.

The Will of this John Porter was dated 24 February 1806 and his son Robert was named as Executor.

Will of John Porter (1736-1806)

Beneficiary	Legacy
Mary (his wife)	£16 per annum for the rest of her life, plus all the linen, plate and furniture
John (his son)	6 guineas (£6 and 6 shillings) per annum, plus his coat and waistcoat with silver buttons
Mary (his daughter)	£5 to each of her 8 children upon their 21st birthday
Ann (his daughter)	£50
Robert (his son)	All the rest of his estate

John Porter (1736-1806) was a butcher and appears to have lived his entire life in the hamlet of Toft. He was successful enough to have a Will drawn up with legacies to a number of family members spread over three generations. Following his death in 1806, a sizeable tombstone was erected on his grave in St Andrew's churchyard in Witham on the Hill. Although now badly eroded, the engraving on the stone includes his age, seventy years, and date of his death. John's widow Mary died in 1820 and the parish records reveal that she was eighty-four years old. No gravestone survives for Mary.

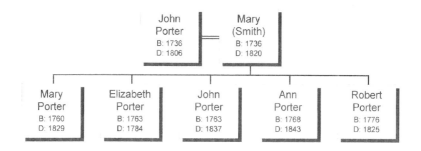

Figure 3.4 Family of John and Mary Porter
A further nine children did not survive infancy. They were Ann (1766),William (1767), Catharine (1770), Francis (1770), William (1771), Fras (1772), Thomas (1774), Mark (1775), and Thomas (1780). All the births and deaths occurred in Toft.

Four children of John Porter (1736-1806) were still living when his Will was signed. These were: Mary (b. 1760), the wife of Robert Turnill; John (b. 1763), the husband of Charlotte Nightingale; Ann (b. 1768), the wife of Robert Cluff; and Robert (b. 1776), who married Mary Halford. A daughter Elizabeth (b. 1763) was John's twin sister but she died at the age of twenty-one. The Will also left a legacy to eight of John's grandchildren, the offspring of Mary Turnill, but failed to name them.

John Porter (1736-1806) had been much better off financially than most of his neighbours and was able to leave enough in his Will to make life easier for all his surviving children and some of his grandchildren. His son Robert had been employed by their father in the butchering trade and inherited this successful business, together with the butchering tools and premises in 1806. The photograph at Fig. 3.5 shows a few of the buildings in Toft in the late nineteenth century. The house in the centre is Pennine Cottage, to the right is Pensbury Cottage, the Old Butcher's Arms and The Gables. Part of the Old Butcher's Arms is thought to be 400 years old and this is the building John Porter (1736-1806) is believed to have occupied.

Figure 3.5 Toft in the nineteenth century
All these buildings have survived substantially unchanged

Robert Porter continued to run the butcher shop in Toft and also became a licensed victualler. When he died in 1825, at the relatively young age of forty-eight his estate had grown to a much greater value than he himself had inherited. Based upon all the information examined, there is no evidence that the early generations of the Porter family enjoyed anything other than a comfortable, stable existence during the eighteenth and early part of the nineteenth centuries.

We know even more about the next generation. John Porter (1763-1837), the elder brother of Robert the butcher, inherited six guineas (£6 6s 0d) per annum from the Will of his father. He was an agricultural labourer who had spent his youth in Toft but moved to Lound about the time of his marriage to Charlotte Nightingale in 1798.

Figure 3.6 Manor House Farm, Lound

The hamlet of Lound is small yet it receives several mentions in the Domesday Book. Only one very old dwelling survives: the Manor House Farm, a Grade 2 listed building, dating from the seventeenth century. This was constructed of coarse limestone rubble, which was a common building material at the time, and has a Collyweston slate roof. Collyweston slate is not actually slate but limestone quarried nearby and cut to form roofing material. There is no evidence to suggest that any of the Porters or Nightingales ever lived in Manor House Farm. A picture of Manor House Farm, as it appears today, can be seen in Fig.3.6.

Charlotte Nightingale was born in Lound and lived her entire life in that hamlet. Like the Porter family of Toft, the Nightingale family of Lound had been permanently located in the same hamlet since the beginning of the Witham on the Hill parish records. Lound is no more than a mile from Toft, so this marriage reinforces the old saying: Men would travel further to find a cow than they would to find a bride!

Charlotte's father was William Nightingale, who was himself the only one of a family of eight to survive childhood. Her mother was named Bruce Spencer (her mother's maiden surname was Bruce). William Nightingale and Bruce Spencer had four children, but only their daughter Charlotte and one brother lived to adulthood.

Infant mortality rates in Britain were much higher in the early nineteenth century than today. Epidemics of smallpox, cholera, measles, typhus and tuberculosis, had a devastating impact on those who survived the perils of birth. Health problems were even worse in the cities with their rapidly increasing populations, poor sanitation and widespread poverty. The parish records for Witham on the Hill reveal high rates of infant mortality in both the Porter and Nightingale families but poverty does not appear to have been the cause. Parish vestry records normally identify those persons receiving parish relief because they had become impoverished or in difficult circumstances. The vestry records for this parish have survived and are now in the Lincolnshire Archives but they show no parish relief paid to any member of either of these Porter or Nightingale families throughout the period that they lived in either Toft or Lound. We now know, however, that these records disguise an important truth. At least one member of the Porter family needed parish relief, but the parish had a more cunning way of dealing with his problem.

With the exception of Robert, who had accumulated moderate wealth by the time of his death, it appears that the socio-economic status of this family had begun to decline about the beginning of the nineteenth century. Apart from Robert, every male member of the Porter family was employed as an agricultural labourer in the early part of the nineteenth century, a time when there was a shortage of such work. The Enclosure Movement, the agricultural revolution and the recession were all factors that encouraged agricultural labourers throughout the country to migrate.

The Porter family were affected by two of the Enclosure Acts: that for Castle Bytham in 1803 and Witham on the Hill in 1813, the second such Act to regulate land in the latter village. So by the beginning of the nineteenth century the Porter family, along with many others, had lost the protection that a shared communal existence had provided their ancestors. As long as they remained in Lincolnshire, they were now reliant on finding paid employment from others who owned the land.

There was an oversupply of labour and the chances of finding work in another industry were better in the towns and cities. Until 1820 no member of the Porter family felt the need to migrate, but that year things began to change.

JOHN PORTER, THE BEGGAR

John Porter was baptised on 18 August 1799 in Witham on the Hill. He was the firstborn child of John and Charlotte Porter, who were living in Lound. We know relatively little of John's childhood but at the age of fifteen or sixteen he was hired by Joseph Musson, an elderly farmer living in Counthorpe, to work for a year. Musson made a big mistake: this lad was allowed to work one day too many, working the full 365 days for which he was paid a full year's wages. One of the criteria to gain settlement rights in a different parish was continuous employment in that parish for at least a year. Since no parish wanted to take on the financial responsibility for the poor of another parish, labourers were normally hired for a maximum period of 364 days. This blunder did not manifest itself for four years and by then Musson was dead.

In April 1820, following a particularly difficult winter for agricultural labourers, John Porter was arrested in Toft for wandering and begging. He was convicted by a Justice of the Peace, Samuel Edmund Hopkinson, and sent to a House of Correction (the local gaol in Folkingham) for one week. Since Toft is less than a mile from Porter's place of birth in Lound and both hamlets are in the parish of Witham on the Hill, normally the parish would become responsible for feeding and providing shelter for their own inhabitants in time of need. But the Overseers of the Poor in Witham on the Hill had discovered that they could get rid of their obligation to provide relief for John Porter, because he had worked one day too many, four years earlier, in another parish. Samuel Edmund Hopkinson ruled that the hamlet of Counthorpe, in the parish of Castle Bytham, was Porter's last place of legal settlement, so he was transported by a constable to that parish once his week's imprisonment had expired.

A more detailed explanation of the rules governing settlement in a parish can be found in chapter 7. The documents relating to John Porter's conviction for begging and removal to Counthorpe can be found in the Lincolnshire Archives.

JOHN PORTER, THE MARRIED MAN

We know little else about John's adolescence or early adulthood until he married Ann Thimbleby in the Abbey Church at Bourne on Christmas Eve 1822. Ann was the daughter of William Thimbleby and Amy Merilion and some background on both the Thimbleby and Merilion families, whose names imply Viking and Huguenot descent, is given in Chapter 7. [Bourne is also spelled Bourn: spelling was not fully standardised at this date and some variations will be found in the contemporary records cited.]

In 1836 John Porter was employed as a labourer, earning six shillings per week. This was a low wage, but the rates of pay for all agricultural labourers were depressed and John was fortunate to be employed. John's employer, Thomas Steele, was a farmer and surveyor of the local roads.

By then the British economy had been in the doldrums for two decades. None of the chief alternatives open to agricultural labourers were attractive: Accept the low wages on offer and periodic unemployment and remain an agricultural labourer, or migrate, either to another part of the country where employment was available or take a huge gamble by leaving family and friends forever by migrating abroad. The Porter family did not want to leave.

John and Ann Porter lived briefly in Witham on the Hill following their marriage but this did not appear to cause further problems with the parish because he was employed and did not need parish relief. Their first child, a son named John, was baptised there on 14 September 1823 by the curate, the Revd William Tennant. Some time between late 1823 and early 1826, this young family returned to live in Counthorpe.

John and Ann's second son, George, was baptised in the parish of Castle Bytham on 23 July 1826, the first baptism performed in this parish by their new curate, again the Revd William Tennant. The Porter's third son, Charles, was also baptised by Tennant on 27 May 1832. Charles died in 1840, and according to his death certificate he was then aged eleven. If his age at death was accurately recorded, his baptism had been delayed until he was about three years old, which would have been unusual. Normally children were baptised within a few days or weeks of their birth so this delay seems odd.

The Porter's fourth and final child, Frederick, was baptised in September 1836, but several census records and his death registration certificate all suggest that Frederick was born two or three years before his baptism. Perhaps these delayed baptisms indicate that relations between the Porter family and the church establishment in Castle Bytham were not all that cordial.

A possible reason for poor relations between the Porter family and the curate relates to religion. A Methodist church was founded in Castle Bytham in the early 1830s, with construction of their chapel completed in 1836. Surviving records show that virtually all branches of the Porter family were Methodists. Sadly, no record of the names of early members of this church could be found, so it is only possible to speculate that John Porter (b.1799) may have been overly active in his support for Castle Bytham's Methodist church.

What remains curious is that Frederick's eventual baptism was performed by the same man who was preparing his case to prosecute the child's father. Outwardly, William Tennant probably conducted the baptism in much the same fashion as he had earlier when baptising Frederick's brothers. Sunday was the preferred day for baptisms, so with Frederick's baptism on a Monday there could not have been many witnesses. The relationship between the curate and Ann Porter must have been tense. The man baptising her son and seeking to ensure that her child's well-being would be protected was committing her husband to stand trial. All the villagers of Castle Bytham would be aware of the unfolding drama as the date of trial drew closer. The trial was a month away, and the curate's efforts to obtain witness statements had been intense.

Did Ann decide to arrange the delayed baptism at this time in an attempt to mollify the curate's antagonism towards her husband? Had they been reluctant to accept the Anglican rite earlier because they normally worshipped with the Methodists? Had this already annoyed the curate so that he was the more ready to see John as a thief? If by presenting the child for baptism Ann was now trying to win his sympathy, she was not successful.

THE REVD WILLIAM TENNANT, THE PROSECUTOR

The curate, William Tennant, was born into a modest family in Bentham, Yorkshire, in 1792, but received a first-class education, graduating in 1815 from Pembroke College, Cambridge. That year he was appointed curate of two small, adjoining rural parishes in Lincolnshire: Witham on the Hill and Careby, but he was an able and ambitious man. The following year he became curate of the Parish of Edenham as well. He would soon have met and got to know most of the inhabitants of each of his parishes. The parish records show that he began conducting baptisms, marriages and burials in Witham on the Hill in October 1815 and continued until his departure in 1826.

For some reason Tennant never attained a more senior position within the church than curate. For a clergyman with wealthy connections and himself well off this was unusual. However, from the time he left the parishes of Witham on the Hill, Edenham and Careby, Tennant's power and influence was never dependent upon his rank in the church.

Tennant's status in the community was greatly enhanced by his marriage to Katherine Hopkinson in 1819. Whether Katherine was related to Samuel Edmund Hopkinson, the Justice of the Peace that dealt with John Porter for begging in 1820, is not known, but she was the daughter of the local squire in Careby, Henry Hopkinson. Henry had been High Sheriff of Lincolnshire and was extremely wealthy. When he died in 1825, a sizeable portion of his estate passed to his son-in-law, the Revd William Tennant.

Since much of Tennant's inherited property was situated in the Parish of Castle Bytham, he managed in 1826 to transfer his employment from the parishes of Witham on the Hill, Edenham and Careby and became curate of Castle Bytham and the adjacent Parish of Little Bytham exactly one year after the death of his father-in-law.

It appears that with his Hopkinson connections and his newfound wealth, Tennant was able to build strong business relationships with other wealthy families and local landowners, in particular, the Birch Reynardson family. The full extent of Tennant's business dealings are now impossible to establish but, because of the prominence of those he was dealing with, many legal documents, deeds and wills survive in the National Archives and various county archives confirming that William Tennant was not only acting as the agent for wealthy neighbours, but was also a party acting on his own behalf on many transactions of substantial value.

> *Sacred to the memory of Henry Hopkinson, Esq., only son of William Hopkinson and Elizabeth his wife, who departed this life July the 17, 1825, in the 71 year of his age. He served the office of High Sheriff in the county of Lincoln in the year 1799. This monument of their affection was erected by his seven surviving daughters.*
>
> Wall Plaque in Castle Bytham Church

The large collection of documents relating to the Birch Reynardson family of Holywell found at Lincolnshire Archives, for example, includes title deeds to property in several counties, along with letters, commissions and other papers relating to the public business of this family. These demonstrate just how close the business dealings of the Revd William Tennant had become with the wealthy and influential Reynardson family. In the 1841 census, Tennant and his family can be found living in Castle Bytham. The census reveals that there were seventeen people living in his household: Tennant, his wife, six of their children, eight servants and a young clergyman.

The National Archives also contain documents relating to the winding up of Tennant's own estate following his death in 1849. Part of his estate was conveyed in trust for Jemima Reynardson and another portion for a marriage settlement for Ann Reynardson. Tennant's wealth, although small by Reynardson standards, was unlikely to have been accumulated from his ecclesial duties or from the fees due to him personally. It seems more likely that he acquired wealth through working closely with wealthy neighbours and his wife's family and handling certain important business affairs on their behalf.

HEATHCOTE AND JOHNSON, THE JUDGES

The parish of Witham on the Hill encompassed the village of that name together with three hamlets: Manthorpe, Toft and Lound. The *White's History, Gazetteer & Directory* (1842) describes Witham on the Hill as:

> a pleasant village on a bold eminence, 7 miles N. by W. of Stamford, and 4 miles S.W. of Bourn, has in its township 235 souls and 2093 A[cres] of land, including about 200 acres of woods. Its parish comprehends the townships of Toft-with-Lound, and Manthorpe. Witham Hall, a neat mansion with pleasant grounds, is the seat of Major General William Augustus Johnson, who is lord of the manor, impropriator [a layman who receives the benefit of the church tithe], and owner of all the soil, except three farms...
>
> ... Toft-with-Lound, two hamlets, from 3 to 4 miles S.W. of Bourn, form a township, in the Parish of Witham on the Hill, containing 225 souls, and 1370 acres of land, belonging to General Johnson, General Reynardson, Sir Gilbert Heathcote and several smaller owners.

In 1793, at the age of sixteen, William Augustus Johnson had purchased a commission in the British Army. He had served during the Peninsular Wars and was present at the battles of Rolica, Vimiero and Corunna. He inherited a large estate at Witham on the Hill from an uncle in 1814 and retired from the army to run this estate. Johnson served as Member of Parliament for Boston 1820-1826 and for Oldham in Lancashire 1837-1847. He was a Magistrate, Deputy Lieutenant of Lincolnshire and Northamptonshire, and became High Sheriff of Lincoln in 1839.

Like General Thomas Birch Reynardson and Sir Gilbert Heathcote, Major General William Augustus Johnson had a major role at the trial. As the local Squire, he would take his place on the bench as Chairman of the Justices.

CHAPTER 4

CRIME AND PUNISHMENT

Britain's unemployment problem in the early nineteenth century helped stimulate a massive migration from the countryside to the new industrial towns and cities. Although work was available, wages in the mills and factories were desperately poor and a large segment of the population had difficulty in making ends meet. Many resorted to petty crime to feed their families and for some it became a way of life. Criminality also increased in rural areas where the theft of livestock had become a sensitive issue.

THE CRIME

During the night of Saturday, 6 August 1836, someone entered a wooded area in the parish of Castle Bytham and slaughtered a sheep, but removed only the hind legs. The carcass was then taken into an open field, where the still warm remains were discovered by John Pretty, a local farmer, the following morning. With the fleece remaining on the carcass, the dead animal's owner would not be difficult to find.

John Pretty went straight to the owner, the Revd William Tennant, curate of Castle Bytham. Pretty would later testify that the animal had been killed, in a very unskilful manner, in Cabbage Hill Wood which lies midway between the village of Castle Bytham and the hamlet of Counthorpe (see Fig. 4.1), then dragged to Dobhill Close, an open field nearby. The culprit was clearly inexperienced at slaughtering sheep and naive at covering his tracks. Surely a professional sheep stealer would have hidden the fleece, or at least have removed the identifying markings, and have left the carcass in the woods rather than drag it into the open. Perhaps the felon was a lunatic!

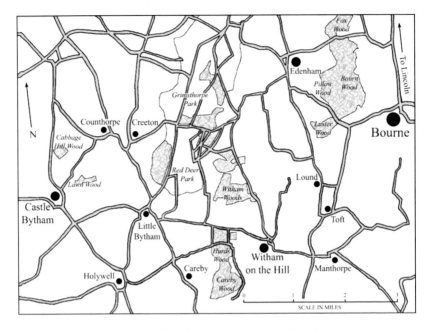

Figure 4.1 Map showing the scene of the crime
Cabbage Hill Wood is midway between Castle Bytham and Counthorpe

The Revd William Tennant's actions over the following week portray a man who was certain that he knew the culprit's identity. He focused his attention on just one person, John Porter, aged thirty-seven, a labourer living in Counthorpe. Tennant had known John Porter for over twenty years and Ann, his wife, for over twelve. In a small parish like Castle Bytham, the curate was bound to know everyone: perhaps the Porters were not his favourite parishioners. The theft of a sheep was a serious matter requiring swift and effective action, so Tennant immediately set about collecting witness statements.

However, Tennant had a problem; no-one had actually witnessed the crime. Yes, Porter had served a week in gaol for begging sixteen years earlier. People reliant on employment in agriculture sometimes went hungry and resorted to begging and local people would know that he had merely been a pawn in a cost reduction exercise between parishes. There is no evidence of any previous involvement in crime. Perhaps there were other factors that persuaded Tennant that he had his man!

PREPARING FOR TRIAL

By Monday, 15 August, following a week of energetic preparation, Tennant was ready. He travelled to Bourne, six miles east of Castle Bytham, but he was not alone. Accompanying him was a widow, Mary Alice Spridgen, and a married woman, Mary Hodson, both residents of Counthorpe, as well as the farmer, John Pretty of Castle Bytham. Each of the curate's travelling companions was prepared to give statements under oath in Bourne to a Justice of the Peace, Thomas Birch Reynardson, who happened to have long established and significant business dealings with Tennant.

Tennant must also have confronted his suspected felon because also arriving in Reynardson's office that day was the accused, John Porter, who gave a voluntary statement basically stating his whereabouts on the afternoon and evening of Saturday, 6 August, and the following two days. Porter claimed he had gone to Bourne on 6 August to visit his mother-in-law who was ill, then purchased some mutton in the market at Bourne. He also mentioned that he had gone to Lound, a hamlet in the Parish of Witham on the Hill, the following Monday, the day of the Lound feast.

LOUND FEAST

Monday, 8 August 1836 was Feast Day in Lound. Feast, an ancient term for 'festival', meant that almost all the population of such a tiny hamlet would attend and some from further afield might participate as well. Feast Days were usually held on the Saint's day of the local parish church and Lound's may well have originally had religious significance but by 1836, with a population of less than sixty souls and just fourteen dwellings, Lound was far too small to warrant its own parish church or even a chapel of ease. But none of this mattered to the people gathered in Lound that summer's day: They had come to enjoy themselves.

4.2 Feast Day

Lound Feast had become an event for the community. There would probably have been games and races for the children, displays and perhaps competitions for local garden produce and handicrafts.

A Feast day offered the whole community a short break from the drudgery of everyday life: These community events were intended to be fun and those that could attend were likely to be well fed. A few years later, after the invention of reproducible photography, posed photo sessions were sometimes included in the day's activities, such as the one in Swinstead, a parish about ten miles north west of Witham on the Hill, taken about half a century later (see Fig. 4.2).

Among those celebrating were an elderly couple, John Porter (1763-1837) and his wife Charlotte, née Nightingale, long-time residents of Lound. All ten of their children had been born in Lound and their eldest son John (b.1799), a resident of Counthorpe, made the four-mile journey on foot to visit his parents, brothers and sisters and attend the Feast. While in Lound, enjoying the feast, John was given some meat by his mother to take home to his family, but this gift would play an almost immediate and devastating part in the life of John Porter, his wife and their young sons. Two days earlier, a sheep had been slaughtered six miles away and its owner was furious.

The Statements

John Porter's statement contains a reference to obtaining some beef and mutton while in Lound but this statement does not make clear who provided the mutton. His statement can be seen in full in the trial documents (which appear later in this chapter), along with the three statements of Mary Hodson, Mary Alice Spridgen and John Pretty, all signed on 15 August. The Justice of the Peace, T.B. Reynardson, had the power to commit John Porter to trial there and then but, based on the information presented, he chose not to do so. The prosecutor's case appears almost farcical, resting on a neighbour's cat seen dragging a bone from the direction of Porter's house. Reynardson probably suggested to his business associate that better evidence was required. So Tennant set about improving his case.

Eight days later, Tennant was back in front of Reynardson in Bourne. Again he was not alone. Mary Alice Spridgen and Mary Hodson both made additional statements, which had both to be amended before either woman was prepared to sign. The 'before and after' versions of these statements can be seen later in this chapter. John Pretty also returned to Bourne but did not amend his original statement. Thomas Steel, John Porter's employer, added a new statement. The statements given by these two men were purely factual and did not implicate the accused, while the two women witnesses had completely new stories to tell. They recount the odd behaviour of Ann Porter, reporting that she was knitting late at night and washing at an early hour and her husband John was reported to have been fetching water. Yet, again these statements contain nothing which ties John to the crime.

Then Tennant submitted his own statement. However, by now he had seen the contents of Porter's statement given a week earlier and in the meantime had taken his investigations further by visiting the accused's parents, John and Charlotte Porter, at their home in Lound.

The Porter and Nightingale families had been residents of Lound for decades. Tennant would have known them well, having previously served as curate in their parish for eleven years. The accused's father was seventy-four years old and his mother sixty-two. Tennant's purpose in visiting was to quiz them on their son's activities on the day of the Lound Feast and his statement, sworn two days after this visit, states that the parents told him they did not give their son mutton but that they did give him some beef. The parents played no part in the trial of their son, so Tennant's version of what the parents were alleged to have told him was never challenged nor verified in court.

When the four statements of Hodson, Spridgen, Steel and Tennant had been sworn before the magistrate, Thomas Birch Reynardson, on 23 August 1836, he agreed to issue committal proceedings, but on condition that Tennant be liable for recognisance of £50 and the other witnesses be liable for £20 each, should they not turn up in court to testify. This was standard court procedure and the court documents show that they all attended. The state would not act as prosecutor in this case, so Tennant had to bring it to court as a private prosecution.

Once the committal had been signed, the court issued a warrant and John Porter would have been arrested. Felons awaiting trial in Kesteven were imprisoned in the House of Correction in Folkingham, nine miles north of Bourne (see Fig. 4.3). The trial was scheduled to take place in Bourne at the next General Quarter Sessions; the whole of the 17th and 18th of October was set aside to hear the eighteen cases scheduled for those Quarter Sessions. Provision was made to continue cases the following week if any could not be completed within those two days.

The record of the trial of John Porter of Counthorpe at the Kesteven Quarter Sessions on 18 October 1836, is one of a number of convict cases that can be found in Lincolnshire Archives. The Quarter Sessions were the middle-ranking court that dispensed justice for the area. The lowest level cases would be heard in the Magistrates Court, while the most serious cases, such as murder, would go to the Assizes. All of the surviving documentation for this trial has been transcribed and can be found later in this chapter.

Whatever conclusions the reader reaches regarding the verdict and sentence, they are reminded that British justice in the nineteenth century was harsh and often operated in this way. Transportation to a penal colony meant virtually certain exile for the rest of the convict's life. There were many thousands of similar cases, all with life-changing consequences for both the convicted and their family members, who needed to adapt quickly. The forced absence of the breadwinner for the rest of his or her life condemned some of those left behind to lives of misery.

Figure 4.3 House of Correction at Folkingham

AN INTERLUDE

August 1836 had been an exciting month in the parish of Castle Bytham and preparations for the trial were well advanced before the month ended. Could September produce more drama?

With John Porter locked up in the House of Correction in Folkingham, the Revd William Tennant was able to return to his duties as curate and attend to his other affairs. On behalf of the parish, he presided over two events of passing interest to the pending trial. One was the baptism of the defendant's son, Frederick. The other was the remarriage of Mary Alice Spridgen.

Mary Alice Spridgen was a widow with two young children. Her husband James had died sixteen months earlier. She was an active lady, perhaps a little too active and she had a problem. In her second witness statement, Mary Alice remembered staying up throughout the night to observe the behaviour of her neighbours, the Porters. She wanted to be helpful to her curate over the loss of his sheep, and when the story of the cat didn't seem to achieve adequate credibility, widow Spridgen produced a new story, no doubt intending to be even more helpful.

As was common in those days, widows often remarried quickly, but Mary Alice was not quick enough: in August 1836 her pregnancy was already beginning to show. However, with Tennant officiating, Mary Alice Spridgen was able to marry a bachelor, Thomas Robinson, a somewhat younger resident of Counthorpe on 3 October 1836 in the parish church in Castle Bytham. A fortnight after her marriage, the newly-wed Mrs Robinson would make her way to Bourne to testify at the trial of her neighbour. On 6 January 1837 Mr and Mrs Robinson would call on the Revd William Tennant to perform another service, the baptism of Mary Alice's newborn son, Thomas.

THE TRIAL

Petty crimes were common in late eighteenth and early nineteenth century England, but for a civilised country punishments were draconian. For example, a sentence of seven years penal servitude followed by a further seven years of police supervision was given to John Walker, an agricultural labourer living in Beeston, Bedfordshire, for stealing some onions valued at less than five shillings. Another example involved fourteen-year-old Henry Catlin who lived in Bedford. He stole three shillings and six pence; his punishment was a fourteen-years sentence and transportation to Van Diemen's Land (later renamed Tasmania). No matter how harsh the sentences, the number of cases tried in court continued to increase during the nineteenth century. Proverty was also increasing and much of the increase in crime stemmed directly from it.

The venue for the trial was Bourne Town Hall, an elegant little building erected in 1821 and it still exists. Two days were set aside to hear all the cases for that Quarter and to conduct all sorts of other business needing court ratification for the Kesteven District.

Figure 4.4 A recent photograph of Bourne Town Hall
The meeting place for Kesteven Quarter Sessions in October 1836

The trial of John Porter of Counthorpe should have started at the Kesteven Quarter Sessions on Monday, 17 October, but the trial of Thomas Moysey, a butcher living in Toft, occupied the court for the whole of that day, so Porter's trial did not begin until Tuesday morning, 18 October 1836. Moysey was also accused of sheep stealing but, unlike the Porter case, there was damning evidence against Moysey. The local constable had been dispatched to Moysey's butcher shop in Toft and discovered the fleece of the stolen sheep on his premises. The corresponding evidence in the Porter case was Mrs Hodson's cat, seen dragging a mutton bone from the direction of the Porters' house.

John Porter's grandfather had been a butcher in Toft, but he had died thirty years earlier. Porter's uncle, Robert Porter, had inherited the butcher shop, so John would have been exposed to the butchering trade in his youth. It is therefore likely that John Porter would have known how to slaughter an animal properly and how to dress the meat. But Uncle Robert had been dead for twelve years when this crime was committed and no-one in the Porter family had been a butcher since then.

It is unlikely that there were any links between the Porter and Moysey cases, but since they were for the same offence, one wonders if there was confusion in juror's minds caused by these cases being heard one after the other. By the end of the first day, the verdict in the Moysey trial finally came: Guilty. The sentence was life imprisonment.

By the standards of the time, both trials occupied the court for longer than usual. Porter's trial occupied the whole morning of the second day and ended at two o'clock in the afternoon. Two local newspapers covered both the Porter and Moysey trials but neither newspaper adds anything to the evidence contained in the witness statements. The Moysey trial documents can also be found at the Lincolnshire Archives.

John Porter told the court that he was a labourer, employed by Thomas Steel of Castle Bytham. The court heard that Porter's parents lived at Lound, that his wife's name was Ann, and that his wife's parents lived in Bourne. The court records noted that John Porter was able to read and write imperfectly but we know that he was unable to sign his own marriage certificate or his own witness statement. It is highly unlikely that John Porter ever attended school and he, like most other agricultural labourers at that time, would only have had the most basic education or literacy skills at best.

The prosecutor in the case of John Porter was the Revd William Tennant himself. It was common for the victim of a petty crime such as this to prosecute his own case and, as the witness statements show, Tennant set about this task with gusto. For some reason John Porter was foolish enough to provide a voluntary statement, which gave two alleged sources for his acquisition of mutton at the time of the crime.

Tennant tried to discredit one source by claiming that Porter's mother gave him no mutton but beef instead. In fact, John Porter never claimed that his mother gave him mutton, but the court seemed happy to rely only

Figure 4.5 Bourne Market
Bourne Town Hall can be seen on the right

on Tennant's word without calling John Porter's parents to confirm or deny Tennant's version. The other source claimed by Porter was his purchase of mutton from a vendor in the market at Bourne, but this appears to have been overlooked by the court. Instead, the prosecution case may have depended solely upon such hearsay as the actions of a neighbour's cat or Mrs Ann Porter doing domestic chores at odd hours. One of the newspapers reporting the outcome of the trial, *The Lincoln Chronicle* in the 21 October 1836 edition, added a curious snippet of news when reporting the Moysey and Porter trials. It reads:

> Bourne Sessions was protracted to Tuesday evening owing to the quantity of business. The court was occupied a considerable portion of Monday with the long and interesting trial to conviction of Thomas Moysey of Toft, butcher, for stealing a fat sheep from Mr. S. Hotchkin, of Rippingale; and on Tuesday the trial to conviction of John Porter of Counthorpe, labourer, for slaughtering a sheep

belonging to Rev. Wm. Tennant, of Castle Bytham, occupied the court until 2 o'clock... Moysey and Porter were sentenced to transportation for the rest of their natural lives.

This was the account of the Porter and Moysey trials as contained in that newspaper, but the editor chose to follow it immediately with the following:

An animal, resembling, in some respects, a dog, has been seen several times lately in the Parish of Bourn. It is described as being beautifully spotted and striped, and about the size of a terrier. Some sheep in the neighbourhood of the wood, have, it is said, been worried by this nondescript.

Whether this newspaper editor was subtly poking fun at the court, or suggesting another cause of death for the sheep, we shall never know!

The trial judges were William Augustus Johnson Esq., and Gilbert John Heathcote Esq., both prominent local landowners. The book, *A Piece of the Puzzle* (Witham-on-the-Hill Historical Society, 2000), describes Johnson as controlling village life and relishing his position of squire. In addition to his many other prominent positions, he was also Chairman of Kesteven Quarter Sessions.

The other judge, Gilbert John Heathcote, Baronet, held the title Lord of the Manor for Witham on the Hill, but his properties were spread over several parishes. The jury consisted of one miller, one brewer, one grazier and nine farmers. The prosecutor, Tennant, was educated at Cambridge University and had become moderately wealthy. If sheep stealing was becoming a problem for local land owners in general at this time, it would obviously be in the interest of them all to stamp it out quickly and effectively.

So when John Porter entered court he faced judges and jurors with a strong interest in deterring any more theft of livestock. As a group they were wealthy, powerful and educated men. The defendant, an agricultural labourer, had none of these advantages, nor was he represented by anyone to argue his defence. With the court unwilling to challenge any of the witness statements, preferring to rely on the comical evidence of a neighbour's cat, was the verdict a foregone conclusion?

The trial of John Porter was just one on a list of eighteen trials scheduled for Kesteven Quarter Sessions in October 1836. Once Moysey's trial had taken up the whole of the first day the court was under pressure to get through all the remaining cases.

At the beginning of the trial, John Porter pleaded 'not guilty', but the jury found otherwise. Another newspaper reported both the verdicts:

> John Porter of Counthorpe, labourer, aged 40, found guilty of feloniously slaughtering one ewe sheep, the property of the Reverend William Tennant of Castle Bytham, and stealing therefrom the two hind legs, was sentenced to be transported for life, pursuant to the statute.

> Thomas Moysey of Toft, butcher, aged 34, found guilty of stealing one wether sheep, the property of Mr. Edmund Hodgekin, of Kirkby Underwood, farmer, was sentenced to be transported for life.
>
> *Lincoln Chronicle & General Advertiser*
> 21 October 1836 page 3 col.2

Serious questions remain over the fairness of the trial, but what about the severity of these sentences? Other cases, in fact thousands of other cases, show that these sentences were by no means unusual at the time. They serve to demonstrate how the rich and influential treated the poor and weak. It is part of what Shakespeare meant by 'the insolence of office' (*Hamlet*, Act III Scene 1).

Transported, but to where? The court did not have the power to select the penal colony, so Porter and Moysey would have to wait to learn their destination. But both would have known that it really did not matter: they would end up somewhere on the other side of the world and would never see England again.

The sentences specified that both Porter and Moysey were to be taken immediately to Folkingham House of Correction, then shortly thereafter moved to the gaol in Lincoln Castle. Later still, the pair would be taken to one of the prison hulks moored in the Thames in London, there to wait for the ship that would take them to some unknown distant place.

The trials of Porter and Moysey now over, the landowners of Kesteven might even believe that they had deterred other would-be sheep stealers.

SOME UNANSWERED QUESTIONS

Examination of the documentation relating to the Porter case raises some questions:

1   Why were John Porter's parents not called to give evidence? The prosecution's case relied on the Revd William Tennant's statement that the parents gave their son 'no mutton'.

2   Given the value of the sheep, twenty shillings (£1 - one pound), and assuming Porter was guilty, why was there not some effort made to obtain payment for the sheep before trial? Tennant would know that if a breadwinner, such as John Porter, was convicted a much more costly burden was likely to fall upon the parish in poor relief to support his family.

3   On the second day of the Kesteven Quarter Sessions, when Porter was also found guilty, the Justices, William Augustus Johnson and Gilbert John Heathcote, did not make out separate sentencing papers against Porter, but merely added his name to Thomas Moysey's sentencing document issued the preceding day. Did the Justices and Jury think the Moysey and Porter cases were connected?

4   Why was Robert Bowder not called to give evidence? He was a grocer and butcher in Castle Bytham and Tennant's statement alleged that Porter visited him just before and just after the sheep was slain? Surely his testimony would have been relevant.

5 Was Tennant acting solely on his own behalf in prosecuting this case? All the officials and almost all the jurymen in court on 18 October 1836 would have had a vested interest in convicting sheep stealers and dealing harshly with them.

Figure 4.6 Robert Bowder's store in Castle Bytham
For many years this was in the stone building on the left of this recent photograph

Tennant remained curate of Castle Bytham and neighbouring parishes until his death in 1849, conducting his final baptismal service in Castle Bytham in December 1848. Following his death a large part of his estate was sold to Mrs Reynardson, the widow of his business associate and wealthy neighbour, Thomas Birch Reynardson, who had died two years earlier. One may wonder whether Tennant, with his new-found wealth and strong business relationships with local landowners, was among those clergy who abused their position. Does he fit Hylson-Smith's characterization (see chapter 2) as the 'corrupt and bloated lackey of the unreformed system'?

THE TRIAL DOCUMENTS

I   Initial Statements

I.1. John Pretty's statement, 15 August 1836

The Parts of Kesteven
In the County of Lincoln

The Information and Complaint of John Pretty of the Parish of Castle Bytham, Yeoman taken upon Oath before me, the undersigned, one of his Majesty's Justices of the Peace in and for the said Parts, this Fifteenth day of August in the year of our Lord 1836

Who saith, That on Sunday Morning the 7th Instant he found in Dob Hall Close near Cabbage Hill Wood in Castle Bytham aforesaid the Carcass of a Ewe Sheep (3 shearling) the property of Rev. William Tennant warm with the legs cut off and carried away and the skin and remainder of the Carcass left - it appeared to have been slaughtered in the Wood in the Close and taken to the spot where found about four or five yards off - it was slaughtered very unskillfully, very badly done - the head was nearly off, the windpipe cut much further than it need be. Mr. Tennant showed Informant a bit of mutton this Morning which in this Informant's judgment appears to have been taken from the middle of the leg.

Sworn Before me   (the Signature of) **John Pretty**
T Birch Reynardson

This statement is in Tennant's handwriting

I.2 Mary Alice Spridgen's statement, 15 August 1836

The Parts of Kestevan
In the County of Lincoln

The Information of Mary Alice Spridgen
of the Township of Counthorpe in the said Parts, Widow
taken upon Oath before me, the undersigned, one of His Majesty's
Justices of the Peace in and for the said Parts,
this Fifteenth day of August, in the year of our Lord, 1836

Who saith, That On Wednesday Morning last she saw Mrs. Hodson's Cat run past with a large bit of mutton from the direction of John Porter's home and this Informant's son James said to her that he saw the Cat come out of Porter's home with it.

Sworn Before me: (signature of) **Mary Alice Spridgen**
T. Birch Reynardson

This statement is in Tennant's handwriting

Figure 4.7
How do you plead?

I.3 Mary Hodson's statement, 15 August 1836

The Parts of Kesteven
In the County of Lincoln

The Information of Mary Hodson, wife of George Hodson
Of the Township of Counthorpe in the said Parts, Labourer
taken upon Oath before me, the undersigned, one of his Majesty's
Justices of the Peace in and for the said Parts, this Fifteenth day of
August in the year of our Lord 1836

Who saith, That On Wednesday Morning last, Ann the wife of John Porter who lives next door came to her house and said this Informant's Cat had got her meat - this Informant saw her Cat come with two bits of Mutton and she found upon looking about the two bits in her garden near where the Cat has a kitten She examined the same which she found to be Mutton - it smelt sour as if it had not been properly bled - it was full of fly blows and was part of a leg - on one bit there were the things of the tendon - they were given up to Mr. Cook by her husband. She also saw the bone of a leg of Mutton in Mr. Steel's Close opposite Porter's house. Ann Porter said her husband had cut off the meat for her to clean the fly blows and also that her husband had brought it from Lound feast.

Sworn Before me:　　　　　　(The mark of) **Mary "X" Hodson**
T. Birch Reynardson

This statement is in Tennant's handwriting

I.4 John Porter's statement, 15 August 1836

The Parts of Kesteven in the County of Lincoln

The Voluntary Examination of John Porter of Counthorpe
in the said Parts and County, Laborer
charged with slaying a sheep belonging to the Rev. William Tennant
taken before me Thomas Birch Reynardson Esquire
one of his Majesty's Justices of the Peace
this Fifteenth day of August 1836

Who saith "After receiving my Money, viz, Six shillings from my Master Mr. Steel on Saturday afternoon the 6th August Instant I started from Counthorpe at half past Three and went to Bourn hearing my Wife's Mother was ill and there bought a bit of Mutton, about Two pounds of a stranger who undersells other people in Bourn Market and gave him a Shilling for it, but do not know his name - he comes from Sleaford way. I came back to Counthorpe about Six O'Clock and went to Bed betwixt Eight and Nine. My Wife and Children went to Bed at the same time - the next morning at between Six and Seven I went to Bowder's at Castle Bytham and returned home about Eight O'Clock. On Monday last, I went to Lound Feast about Eight in the morning to my Father's and returned at night and brought back a bit of Mutton undressed about a Pound or a Pound and a half and two bits of boiled Beef which my Mother gave me.

The Mark of
John "X" Porter

Taken and subscribed
Before me
T. B. Reynardson

This statement is in Reynardson's handwriting

II   Additional Statements

II.1 Mary Alice Spridgen's Additional Statement, 23 August 1836

Mary Alice Spridgen
Additional Statement
Original Version

23 August 1836. The said Mary Alice Spridgen Being Sworn, Saith, That she went to the house of John Porter on Saturday the 6th August Instant and remained there from the hour of Twelve midnight up to the hour of 2 in company with Porter's wife and Porter was not there all the time she this Informant stayed there and Informant then went home.

This Statement was altered to the version that appears below.

Additional Statement
Amended Version

23rd August 1836. The said Mary Alice Spridgen Being Sworn, Saith, That she went to the door of the house of John Porter on Saturday the 6th August Instant and observed there John Porter's wife knitting by Candlelight at night at the hour of Twelve midnight. Informant said to her "are you not gone to bed yet" and Porter's wife made no answer but went upstairs. Porter himself was not there and Informant then went home. Said Informant spoke to John Porter at his own house door at half past five in the afternoon of Saturday 6th August.

Sworn Before me: (signature of) **Mary Alice Spridgen**
T. Birch Reynardson

This statement is in Tennant's handwriting

II.2 Mary Hodson's Additional Statement, 23 August 1836

Mary Hodson
Additional Statement
Original Version

23ʳᵈ August 1836 The said Mary Hodson being sworn Saith: That she believes from what she observed that John Porter and his wife were up most part of Saturday night. That she heard towards break of day a noise of chopping at their house. That at six in the morning on Sunday the 7ᵗʰ August Porter's wife was washing the house and the goods were placed out of doors which was not usually done by her at other times.

That she saw John Porter fetching water on the Sunday night at about nine o'clock. He was also fetching water on Monday night at about nine o'clock and again fetching water on Tuesday night. That John Porter came home on the Sunday night about nine o'clock and waited at Mrs. Spridgen's until his wife's return home from Castle Bytham.

This statement was altered to the version that appears below.

Additional Statement
Amended Version

23ʳᵈ August 1836 The said Mary Hodson being sworn Saith: That she believes from what she observed that John Porter and his wife were up most part of Saturday night the 6ᵗʰ August Instant. That she heard a frapping about and heard towards break of day a noise of chopping at their house. That she saw a light in their house at 10 that night and her husband observed there was a light at 11. That at six in the Morning on Sunday the 7ᵗʰ August Porter's wife was washing the house and the goods were placed out of doors which was not usually done by her at other times.

II.2 Mary Hodson's Additional Statement, continued

That she, this Informant, saw John Porter fetching water on the Sunday night at about Nine o'Clock. He was also fetching water on Monday night at about nine o'clock and again fetching water on Tuesday night at about 8 o'Clock. That John Porter came home on the Sunday night at about 9 o'clock and waited at Mrs. Spridgen's until his wife's return home from Castle Bytham.

Sworn Before me: (the Mark of) **Mary "X" Hodson**
T. Birch Reynardson

This statement is in Tennant's handwriting

II.3 William Tennant's Additional Statement, 23 August 1836

The Parts of Kesteven
In the County of Lincoln

**The information of The Reverend William Tennant
of the Parish of Castle Bytham of the said Parts, Clerk (in Holy
Orders) taken upon Oath before me, the undersigned, one of his
Majesty's Justices of the Peace in and for the said Parts, this
Twenty third day of August in the year of our Lord 1836**

Who Saith That: He suspects John Porter of Counthorpe in the said parts, Laborer, with having feloniously slain a Ewe Sheep his property from a Close called Dobhall Close in Castle Bytham and stolen the legs off the same leaving the skin and the rest of carcass. That he inquired last Monday of the father and mother at Lound of John Porter and they both said that they gave him at Lound Feast on Sunday 7th August Instant a piece of baked beef and a piece of pudding but no Mutton as they had no Mutton.

That Robert Bowder of Castle Bytham, Shopkeeper, told this Informant that John Porter was in his shop about seven o'clock in the evening of Saturday the 6th August and that he went there again on the Sunday morning.

Sworn Before me: (signature of) **Wm. Tennant**
T. Birch Reynardson

This statement is in Tennant's handwriting

II.4 Thomas Steel's Statement, 23 August 1836

The Parts of Kesteven in the County of Lincoln

The Information of Thomas Steel
Of the Parish of Castle Bytham
in the said Parts, Farmer

Taken upon Oath before me, the undersigned,
one of his Majesty's Justices of the Peace In and for the said Parts,
this Twenty Third day of August in the year of our Lord 1836

Who Saith, That John Porter of Counthorpe, Laborer having been employed by this Informant as Surveyor of Counthorpe Roads came to this Informant about the hour of Eight in the Afternoon of Saturday the 6th August Instant at his, this Informant's, house in Castle Bytham and received his wages Six Shillings.

Sworn before me   (signature of) **Thos Steel**
T. Birch Reynardson

This statement is in Tennant's handwriting

III The Trial Documents

III.1 The Recognizance

To Prefer Felony

The Parts of Kesteven
In the County of Lincoln
To Wit.

Be it remembered, that on the Twenty third day of August in the Year of our Lord, One Thousand Eight Hundred and Thirty six, The Reverend William Tennant of Castle Bytham in the said parts, Clerk, Thomas Steel of Castle Bytham aforesaid Farmer, John Pretty of Castle Bytham aforesaid Yeoman, and Mary Alice Spridgen of Counthorpe in the said Parts Widow personally came before me, one of his Majesty's Justices of the Peace for the said Parts of Kesteven and acknowledged himself to our Sovereign Lord the King (that is to say) The said William Tennant the sum of Fifty Pounds and the said Thomas Steel, John Pretty and Mary Alice Spridgen the sum of Twenty Pounds each

Upon Condition, that the said William Tennant shall personally appear at the next General Quarter Sessions of the Peace to be holden in and for the said Parts of Kesteven, and then and there prefer a Bill of Indictment against John Porter late of Castle Bytham aforesaid Laborer for feloniously slaughtering a Ewe Sheep and stealing part of the Carcass on the Sixth day of August at Castle Bytham aforesaid the Property of the said William Tennant and shall then and there give Evidence concerning the same to Jurors, who shall inquire thereof on the part of our said Lord the King: And also in case the same be found a true Bill - then if the said William Tennant and also the said Thomas Steel, John Pretty and Mary Alice Spridgen shall give Evidence on the said Indictment, and not depart the Court without leave. Then this Recognizance shall be void.

III.2 Calendar of Prisoners for Trial

The Parts of Kesteven
In the County of Lincoln

Calendar of Prisoners for Trial at the General Quarter Session of The Peace holden at Bourn in and for the said Parts on Monday the Seventeenth day of October 1836 Before *[left blank]* **Chairman and others his fellows, and Afterwards Continued and held by Adjournment at New Sleaford in and for the said Parts on Friday the Twenty first day of the same Month, Before** *[left blank]* **Chairman and others his fellows,**

Name Age Trade, etc	Offence
John Porter} **40 Laborer imp}**	the oath of Rev Wm Tennant of Castle Bytham with feloniously Slaying a Ewe Sheep and Stealing therefrom the two legs his property.

Notes: This calendar included seventeen other prisoners.

John Porter's age is recorded as forty in the trial documents but he was three years younger. It was not uncommon for the uneducated to lose track of their age.

III.3 The Jury

Jury to Try John Porter
17 Oct 1836

James Gould the Younger of Billingborough, Grazier
William March of Bourn, Brewer
John Beasley of Dyke and Cawthorpe, Farmer
George Bugg of Horbling, Farmer
Thomas Chapman of Hacconby, Miller
John Quincey of Kirkby Underwood, Farmer
John Hunt of Aslackby, Farmer
Edward Eldret of Hacconby, Farmer
Richard Linney of Castle Bytham, Farmer
Turnball Brothwell of Edenham, Farmer
Levi Lay of Swinstead, Farmer
Richard Smith of Carlby, Farmer

The Same Jury Tried

Wm Leverton for a Pound Bread
Francis Dranfrot for a Misdemeanor
John Stokes for Felony

III.4 Witnesses present at the Trial

[Case] **No. 9**

The Rev'd William Tennant, Prosecutor

[Witnesses]
Thomas Steel
John Pretty
Mary Alice Spidgon [*sic*]
Mary Hodson
Thomas William Hopkinson
Thomas Pitts
Charles Woodcock

[Hopkinson, Pitts and Woodcock gave no written statement. Hopkinson was probably related to Tennant's wife, Katherine Hopkinson. Woodcock was a ten-year-old boy living in the Rectory at North Witham]

A True Bill
Pleads Not Guilty
Jury Say Guilty

III.5 The Verdict

The Parts of Kesteven
In the County of Lincoln

To Wit: The Jurors for our Sovereign Lord the King upon their Oath present that John Porter late of Castle Bytham in the Parts of Kesteven in the County of Lincoln, Labourer on the Sixth Day of August in the Seventh year of the Reign of our Sovereign Lord William the Fourth, by the Grace of God of the United Kingdom of Great Britain and Ireland, King Defender of the Faith, with Force and Arms at Castle Bytham aforesaid in the Parts and County aforesaid, one Ewe Sheep, of the value of Twenty Shillings of the Goods and Chattels of one William Tennant then and there being found, then and there willfully and feloniously did kill with a felonious intent to steal part of the Carcass, that is to say, the two hind legs of the said sheep against the form of the statute in such Case made and provided and against the Peace of our said Lord the King, his Crown and Dignity, etc.

The Said: William Tennant, Prosecutor

III.6 The Sentence (for Porter and Moysey combined)

The Parts of Kesteven
in the County of Lincoln

At the General Quarter Sessions of the Peace of our Sovereign Lord the King, held at Bourn, in and for the said Parts, in the first Week after the Eleventh day of October (to wit.) on Monday the Seventeenth Day of October in the Seventh Year of the Reign of our Sovereign Lord William the Fourth, by the Grace of God of the United Kingdom of Great Britain and Ireland King, Defender of the Faith, and in the Year of our Lord One Thousand Eight Hundred and Thirty Six

Before William Augustus Johnson Esq. Chairman, Gilbert John Heathcote Esq. and others, Justices of our said Lord the King, assigned to keep the Peace of our said Lord the King within the Parts aforesaid, and also to hear and determine of and concerning the several Felonies, Trespasses, Contempts and other Misdemeanors committed within the said Parts.

Whereas John Porter (&) Thomas Moysey late of the Parish Castle Bytham (&) Rippingale in these Parts and County Butcher hath been convicted of Felony, for which he is liable by the Laws of this Realm to be Transported,

It is Ordered, adjudged, and determined by this Court and his Majesty's Justices of the Peace here present. That the said Thomas Moysey be Transported as soon as conveniently may be for the Term of his Natural Life, to such Parts, beyond the Seas, as his Majesty by and with the advice of His Privy Council shall direct, pursuant to the Statute in that Case made and provided

III.6 The Sentence continued

And it is Further Ordered, that Sir Edward French Bromhead, Baronet and the Reverend Edward Chaplin, Clerk Two of his Majesty's Justices of the Peace for the said Parts, be and they are hereby appointed to Contract with any Person or Persons for the Transportation of the said Thomas Moysey as above mentioned, and to cause such Sureties to be taken as the Statute directs, and also to order the said Thomas Moysey (&) John Porter to be delivered pursuant to such Contract to the Person or Persons contracting for him, or to his or their Assigns,

And it is Further Ordered, that the said Thomas Moysey (&) John Porter be conveyed by Matthew Edis Maile, Keeper of the House of Correction at Folkingham, in the said Parts, to the Castle at Lincoln, and that William Brocklesby, Keeper of the said Castle at Lincoln, do receive the said Thomas Moysey (&) John Porter into his Custody accordingly, and there safely keep him until he shall be transported pursuant and according to the said Sentence.

By the Court
[*unsigned*]
Clerk of the Peace for the said Parts

Figure 4.8 Police loadng convicts into a Black-Maria (prison van)

CHAPTER 5

TRANSPORTATION

The incarceration of John Porter and Thomas Moysey began with a local gaol, then the county prison, before their removal to one of the prison hulks moored on the Thames in London. These two convicts were lucky because this part of their ordeal was over relatively quickly. Then came their voyage in a convict ship to forced labour in Australia. The ship's doctor left a detailed record of this voyage.

Until the outbreak of war in America in 1775, British convicts were transported to penal colonies in America. Following the Revolutionary War (1775-1783) Britain needed to find new locations to export her criminal population and penal colonies were established in New South Wales and Van Diemens Land (later Tasmania) among others.

FOLKINGHAM HOUSE OF CORRECTION

Prisons of one kind or another have existed in Folkingham since at least the fifteenth century and by the eighteenth Houses of Correction had become places of punishment for minor offenders. Early in the nineteenth century an enlarged House of Correction, or prison, was built at Folkingham to accommodate prisoners from South Kesteven. Folkingham was a small village, located nine miles north of Bourne on the main London to Lincoln road. Prisoners, such as John Porter, awaiting trial at the Quarter Sessions could be locked up for periods of up to three months before trial. Since Porter was indicted on 23 August 1836, he spent nearly two months at Folkingham prior to his trial. In his book, *A History of Folkingham with Laughton and Stow Green*, L.R. Cryer states, 'On a visit to the prison in 1839, Captain Williams, HM Inspector, was very critical of conditions here, particularly of food, medical care and heavy work. The latter he said was excessive, especially punishment on the treadmill.'

All that survives at Folkingham House of Correction today is the original nineteenth-century gateway and governor's house, which date from 1808. It was a moderately sized local prison, accommodating an average of about forty prisoners in 1836. It was in use as a local prison until 1878.

Those convicted of lesser crimes might serve their full term in Folkingham, but for more serious crimes convicts would spend a few days at Folkingham after hearing their sentence then, as soon as appropriate transport could be arranged, they would be transferred to the much larger gaol at Lincoln Castle. Porter and Moysey were transferred to Lincoln on 26 October, so would have spent eight unpleasant days after conviction at Folkingham.

Figure 5.1 Transportation to Folkingham
On short local journeys convicts were transported alongside fare-paying passengers in public carriages. Boxes underneath the seats stored the chains when not in use on prisoners.

LINCOLN CASTLE

The county gaol for Lincolnshire was built within the walls of Lincoln Castle. Construction of the Castle began in 1068, two years after the Battle of Hastings and for 900 years it contained a working prison within its walls. The gaol that accommodated John Porter was built in the eighteenth century. It is now a museum and Lincoln Castle has become a tourist attraction, with the prison complex providing a major part of the permanent display.

Figure 5.2 Main gate to Lincoln Castle

The prisoners in Lincoln gaol included both debtors and felons. Better-off debtors could live in relative comfort in more spacious and heated accommodation and continue to work at their profession by payment to the turnkey for such privileges. Those that could not afford to pay received harsher treatment and had to endure the worst accommodation.

The influence of the church was ever present, even in the prison. Prisoners were required to attend church services twice daily, but instead of sitting in pews were required to stand in private cubicles. These were designed so that prisoners could not see or be seen by other inmates, but the clergyman delivering his sermon could look down on them from his elevated pulpit and they could only look up to him. Sermon themes would include the mending of 'wicked ways, hell and damnation.'

Upon arrival, Porter and Moysey were examined by the prison surgeon and were found to be too foul and dirty to pass his inspection. He ordered them to be bathed and recorded his criticism of the treatment they had received at Folkingham.

On 4 November 1836, William Brocklesby, Governor of the Prison, wrote to William Forbes, the Clerk of the Peace for Sleaford. His letter said,

> I yesterday received an order from the Secretary of State for the removal of all male convicts in my custody. [They are] to be received on board the Justitia hulk at Woolwich, with all convenient speed. I have therefore made arrangements to leave this place on Monday morning at 10 o'clock and shall be in Sleaford at 1 o'clock.
>
> I shall be obliged by your sending me an order for £60 to enable me to move them.
>
> (signed) WILLIAM BROCKLESBY, Keeper

On 7 November Porter, Moysey and six other convicts from Lincoln Castle began their journey to London. The prisoners, chained together inside the prison van, would have bid farewell to their native Lincolnshire that afternoon. Their guards would have slept at inns along the way, while the prisoners slept in the stables. At a cost of £60 for eight convicts, this 140-mile portion of their eventual 10,000-mile journey would have been but a small part of the total cost of transporting each convict to New South Wales. Since the property stolen in the Porter, Moysey and most of the other cases was trivial, it raises questions about the financial burden to the country of sentencing men, women and children to be transported such distances. The next chapter will suggest a reason.

Figure 5.3 Prison chapel at Lincoln Castle

THE HULKS

When the war ships intended for service in the Revolutionary War became redundant, they began to be used as temporary prison accommodation until the prisoners could be placed on vessels capable of undertaking the long voyages to these new penal colonies. With sails, masts, guns and other battle equipment removed, these former warships, now just hulks, were moored in the Thames and at other locations around the coast so that convicted prisoners from all over Britain could be transferred to them while awaiting transportation. In 1836 four hulks were moored at

Figure 5.4 Convict hulks moored at Woolwich
Photograph courtesy of Greenwich Heritage Centre

Woolwich where Britain maintained one of its most substantial military bases. On the southern shore of the Thames, the Woolwich Warren was a maze of workshops, warehouses, barracks, foundries and firing ranges.

The hulks were moored off-shore and the gun ports sealed to help reduce the risk of escape. Because of the isolated position of the hulks, convicts were less able than prisoners ashore to arrange visits from family and friends.

Life on board the hulks was grim. One young prisoner left the following description:

> orders were received for my being passed on with others to the hulks at Woolwich. Quarters were assigned me on board the *Justitia* Hulk. Before going on board we were stripped to the skin and scrubbed

with a hard scrubbing brush, something like a stiff birch broom, and plenty of soft soap, while the hair was clipped from our heads as close as scissors could go. This scrubbing we endured until we looked like boiled lobsters and the blood was drawn in many places. We were then supplied with new 'magpie' suits - one side black or blue and the other side yellow. Our next experience was being marched off to the blacksmith, who riveted on our ankles rings of iron connected by eight links to a ring in the centre, to which was fastened an up and down strap or cord reaching to the waist-belt. This last supported the links, and kept them from dragging on the ground. Then we had what were called knee garters. A strap passing from them to the basils and buckled in front and behind caused the weight of the irons to traverse on the calf of the leg. In this rig-out we were transferred to the hulk, where we received our numbers, for no names were used. My number was 5418 - called 'five four eighteen'.

This account is taken from *Old Convict Days* by William Derricourt

Both John Porter and Thomas Moysey spent about a month on the hulk *Justitia*. The use of the hulks moored in the Thames was intended as a temporary measure, but thousands of convicts were confined on them for months and some for years. They were in use as prisons continuously from 1776 until 1857. The convicts, sometimes up to 500 a day, were put to work as labourers in the arsenal and dockyards at Woolwich and made to improve the river. Fig. 5.4, from the Greenwich Heritage Centre Collection, shows convict hulks moored on the Thames at Woolwich. These are moored off Bell Watergate, a short street that ran up to the river's edge and still exists today. The hulk in the centre is

Figure 5.5 Cells on hulks

believed to be the *Defence*, the last prison ship to remain in service until she suffered a fire in July 1857. The other vessel is the *Unite* hospital ship. The photo is dated 1856-57. The 'magpie suits' and leg irons described by Derricourt can be seen in Fig. 5.6 and Fig. 5.7.

The prisoners were housed on decks with insufficient headroom for the taller men to stand erect. The quality of food given to prisoners was poor, but sometimes the captain of a hulk would allow prisoners to plant vegetables in plots near the Arsenal. Prisoners who died on board the hulks, and there were many, were buried unceremoniously in the marsh near the Arsenal.

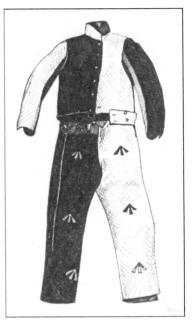

Figure 5.6
Convict Magpie Suit
The Broad Arrows signify British
Government property

Figure 5.7 Convict leg irons
The outside seams on the trousers were not stitched but buttoned so that shackled prisoners could get dressed without removing the leg irons

VOYAGE OF THE *PRINCE GEORGE*

The *Prince George* began to load convicts from two hulks, the *Justitia* and the *Ganymede,* anchored in the Thames in London on 10 December 1836. These two hulks had provided temporary prison accommodation for 130 convicts awaiting transportation to one of His Majesty's Prison Colonies. The *Prince George* then sailed down the Thames to Sheerness and loaded a further 120 convicts from the hulk *Fortitude* anchored at Chatham. The official records of the voyage state that there were 250 prisoners, all male, on board the *Prince George* but the guard consisted of twenty-nine rank and file members of the 80th Regiment under the command of Lieutenant Baxter and Ensign Foster. There were eight women and three children on board.

There was an experienced ship's doctor, Thomas Bell, on board. He had served on four previous convict voyages, transporting prisoners to Australia prior to the sailing of the *Prince George* in 1836-1837. He had been on board the 366-ton vessel, *The Thames,* in 1826 and again in 1829, on the 406-ton *Edward (2)* in 1830, and the 538-ton *Eliza (2)* in 1832. Following his fifth journey as convict ship doctor aboard the *Prince George*, Thomas Bell made a sixth, and final, voyage to Australia, on board the 451-ton barque *Portsea* in 1838.

One of the women passengers was Mary Harp, aged twenty-nine, who was married to one of the guards. She gave birth to a female child three weeks before the voyage began. According to Dr Thomas Bell,

> This unfortunate woman having married without the consent of the commanding officer, although ordered a passage in this ship, is not victualated by government and has laid in no stock of provisions of any kind. It is a great pity that commanding officers of regiments are not more particular in having the women examined by the surgeons of the regiments before they are embarked on convict ships & seeing they are to be properly messed.

Mrs Harp and her baby both died during the voyage, with neglect a major contributory factor, despite Bell's heroic attempts to save their lives.

No record of the number of crew has been found but there would have been over 300 people on board in total, eight of whom did not survive. Six convicts, Mrs Harp and her child were all buried at sea. A summary of this selection of Dr Bell's case records can be found in Appendix A.

The *Prince George* started to leave the Thames on Christmas Day 1836, but that evening encountered a terrific storm, losing both anchors and cables. The vessel, still in the Thames, managed to land at Sheerness. When it was eventually able to return to port, Dr Bell took it upon himself to write to the Admiralty on 27 December (National Archives ADM 101/60/7), pointing out the serious danger of setting off at the very depth of the English winter. Bell's letter was immediately forwarded to Downing Street, suggesting that someone with authority took it seriously. Vessels were, however, still despatched in winter, and convicts may have been at less risk in sailing south, even at the risk of winter storms, than in enduring the British winter on the hulks. Bell also wrote to the commanding officer of Mrs Harp's husband's regiment about Mr Harp's neglect and lack of concern for his wife and child, whose illnesses were brought on by starvation and the want of proper clothing. Why did this soldier not share his food and clothes with his wife and child?

Following repairs, the *Prince George* set off again but put into port at Torbay, either to replenish supplies or to complete the necessary repairs. Then, on 14 January 1837, the voyage to Port Jackson (Sydney) in New South Wales began once again. The Master, Adolphus Holton, planned to make a stop at the Cape of Good Hope, but the winds were against them as they rounded the southern tip of Africa so the voyage continued without stopping. Not stopping at the Cape presented serious risks since provisions and fresh water could be taken on board there and necessary repairs to the ship undertaken. The *Prince George* had a wooden hull which would have leaked to some extent at all times, so constant repairs were essential.

The ship's doctor, Thomas Bell, prepared a detailed report of the voyage which survives at the National Archives at Kew in London (ADM 101/60/7). It appears that all on board the *Prince George* were fortunate to have an experienced and caring physician among them. Bell ordered the removal of leg irons once the vessel was at sea, and initiated daily exercise programmes of walking and dancing. Bell's General Report is partially transcribed later in this chapter, but he also kept a daily record of every treatment administered to each prisoner during their long sea journey. A list of all the names of those who received medical treatment from Dr Bell can be found in Appendix B. This daily record shows that over 75 per cent of the convicts and guards on board received treatment, many of them on several occasions. Dr Bell also prepared case notes on ten of his most serious cases and an abridged summary of these can be found in Appendix A.

From the daily record we learn that John Porter visited the ship's hospital three times during the voyage, twice for dysentery and once for epilepsy. Since no other cases of epilepsy are known in the Porter family, one wonders if Bell's observation of epilepsy in John Porter may have had another cause. For example, this doctor was experimenting with different doses of lime juice mixed with nitre in an attempt to find a remedy for scurvy, and when his supply of nitre ran out, he began to mix lime juice with gunpowder instead.

Whether John Porter's apparent epilepsy was the result of one of Bell's experiments cannot be known, but Bell did manage to arrive in New South Wales after a very long, non-stop voyage having only had three persons die from scurvy, although many suffered from it.

Bell's description of the final few days of the voyage is almost beyond belief. The day before the *Prince George* was set to land in New South Wales she sailed into a 'perfect hurricane' as she was leaving the strait that separates Australia from Van Diemens Land. The terrific violence of this storm, which continued for nearly two full days, tore the sails to shreds and caused significant damage, both inside and outside the ship. The vessel managed to limp into Port Jackson on 8 May 1837, and a remarkably small number, twenty-seven men, needed hospitalisation. There can be little doubt that Bell did a great deal to improve the conditions for the convicts on board the *Prince George* and almost certainly saved many of their lives.

THE FATE OF THE *PRINCE GEORGE*

The sailing ship, *Prince George,* was built in Bristol and entered service in 1830. It was a 482-ton clipper ship operating from the Port of London, carrying cargo back and forth to Bombay until 1836. The *Prince George* transported convicts to Australia only once, on the 1836-1837 voyage, but managed one other commercial voyage to Australia two years later. The vessel continued to operate from London as its home port until 1845, when it transferred to Tyneside in north-east England and sailed from South Shields for the final three years of its active service.

The Master of the *Prince George,* Adolphus Holton, was born in Deal, Kent, in 1808 and eventually became a Master Mariner. It was his maiden voyage as Master of a convict ship when he captained the *Prince George* to Sydney in 1836-1837. He was also Master of convict ships on three further voyages: in 1840 on the 394-ton barque, *Mary Ann III,* in 1845 and again in 1848 on the 611-ton ship, *Mount Stewart.* (Information on the voyages of Thomas Bell and Adolphus Holton is taken from Charles Bateson, *The Convict Ships 1787-1868,* Second Edition 1969).

The *Prince George* needed substantial repairs on three occasions; in 1836 to fit it out for the convict voyage to Australia, in 1838 to repair the damage caused by the hurricane it encountered in May 1837 and finally in 1845, to repair and refit the vessel for voyages between Tyneside and the Mediterranean.

The *Prince George* was listed in *Lloyds Register* continuously from 1831 to 1847 inclusive, but no longer appears from the 1848 edition onwards. There is no record of this vessel being lost, nor is the eventual fate of the *Prince George* listed in *Lloyds Register.* It was therefore just broken up or scrapped because much faster steam-powered vessels were then entering service.

THE REPORT OF THOMAS BELL, SHIP'S SURGEON ON BOARD THE VESSEL *PRINCE GEORGE* 1836-1837

[National Archives ADM 101/60/7. The spelling and underlining is that of the author, Thomas Bell. Subheadings in italics are not original]

GENERAL REMARKS

The Hulks

On the 10th December 1836, 130 male prisoners were embarked at Woolwich from the Justitia and Ganymede Hulks, immediately after their embarkation we proceeded to Sheerness and on the 13th Inst. I went to Chatham to examine the prisoners to be embarked from that Port. On the day following we received 120 Convicts, Cross-Ironed, in consequence of many of them being of desperate character.

In the beginning of Nov'r last, a conspiracy was formed among some of the prisoners of the Fortitude Hulk at Chatham to make their escape. On the morning of the 7th, five of those rose upon the watch and overpowered them, got possession of the Boats then moored to the Ship; they being closely pursued and not sufficient water to float the boats, they jumped to Swim, not having studied the rise and fall of tide, they were astonished to find themselves anchored to the necks in the mud, from which situation they begged hard to be extricated. Seven others had got possession of the main deck; by the prompt assemblage of the officers, and Guard, Aided by the Cook with a red hot poker, were soon driven below. Seven others had their names signed to a paper, and sworn to be true to each other, and to have Death or liberty.

These nineteen men being reported to me by the Government Authorities as desperate characters, coupled with a letter from the Admirals Secretary at Sheerness, stating that the friends and connexions of the Prisoners had been endeavouring to bribe the fishermen and watermen in the neighbourhood to assist them in making their escape, and that the Commanding Officer of the Flagship was made aware of this circumstance &c. Caused me to be more strict and not to allow as many on Deck at a time, while in harbour, as I had hitherto done with other prisoners.

Scurvy

Many of those men were in a low state of health, such as would arise from long confinement, depressed spirits, want of Exercise, despondency and such other debilitating causes. This with a long continuance of Snowy Wet, cold and blowing weather. The loss of Both our Anchors and Cabals [*cables*] on Christmas night, in a most terrific Gale of Wind, and obliged to return to port, Narrowly escaping with our lives, the ship having been driving for several hours, also the fright, Wet, cold and Seasickness those men suffered for the first three weeks after their embarkation, that most of them could take but little nourishment and many until half the voyage was completed could not make use of the Chocolate supplied, although the greatest care was taken in the cooking of it, straining the water &c.

These untoward circumstances no doubt in a great degree conduced to the disease "Scurvy" [or *scorbutus*] that has shewn itself so early and with such virulence on the Voyage.

The first case of Scurvy appeared as early as the 29th of January, the Subject of which, "George Willett" had been a Farmer's Labourer in the low part of Essex, he was of a delicate habit of body and Indolent disposition; came on board in a low state of health, "he says" arising from starvation; For the last two winters being out of employment and provisions high in price, he became very weak for want of food, determined not to die of starvation, Stole a sheep for which he was transported.

Having being supplied with a copy of Mr. Cameron's Pamphlet on Scurvy, which I suppose was intended as a guide to Surgeons in the disease, I was determined to give Nitre in solution with Lime juice a fair trial. It was prepared thus Eight ounces of Nitre were pulverized and mixed with lime juice in the proportion of one drachm of Nitre to one ounce of lime juice, 3gs of the oil of peppermint was diffused in a small quantity of the Spirits of wine [*ethyl alcohol*] to which was added as much sugar as made it palatable. From three to four ounces of this mixture with a little water were given in divided doses from six am until 8.0 pm, increasing or decreasing the quantity as circumstance required; seldom in any stage of the disease giving more than eight ounces in the 24 hours and guarding against any irritation that might be produced of stomach or bowels.

In some cases the acid was largely diluted and mixed with Wine but did not appear to have so good an effect as when given with very little water, or undiluted, with the Nitre &c. Seldom disagreeing with the stomach in the first instance, or in a well-marked case produced any apparent effect on the Abdominal or Urinary organs, although an ounce of Nitre taken in the day.

But in the more advanced cases where the appetite failed, a suitable dilution, and admixture with wine &c, rendered it more palatable, more acceptable, and less offensive to the Stomach. It was occasionally prescribed with the Pulver Cinchona *[powdered bark of the fever tree or Quinine]*; and in some of the worst cases combined with the Sulph. Quinine, in the proportion of 3 or 4 grains, two or three times a day which seemed to increase the appetite and recruit the strength.

Our Nitre being nearly expended, and knowing we had a sufficient quantity of Gunpowder on board, the composition of which is, Six parts of Nitre, with one part of Sulphur and one of Charcoal, and that if Gunpowder be boiled in water the Nitre dissolves, on evaporating the filtered liquor, all the nitre that was in the powder is obtained by crystallization, the Sulphur and charcoal remaining on the filtre. By this easy method I was enabled to get a fresh supply of Nitre. - To some of the patients, the Gunpowder was given in the same proportion as the nitre 3 pts to 3 pts of lime juice.

I cannot say that I could perceive any particular effect produced from the administration of the Nitre first given, that obtained from the Gunpowder, or the gunpowder itself. In some cases after the use of the Lime juice prepared as in the first instance for six or 8 days, the salt provisions being withdrawn, and a Generous diet with wine given, the symptoms gradually disappeared, the medicine was continued for some days longer, the patient being put on the half diet scorbutic list.

[Dr Bell's report continues with a series of detailed medical reports on a variety of conditions that the prisoners presented. These can be found in Appendix C. The text of the General Remarks continues below.]

GENERAL HEALTH: HYGIENE AND EXERCISE

The most strict attention was paid to the comfort, and cleanliness of their persons, and wearing apparel, throughout the voyage. When the weather became warm the prisoners bathed in the mornings, having three tubs for the purpose, every part of the surface was properly cleansed, aided by persons appointed with brushes, the person after coming out of the bath, well rubbed with a hard, dry, towel, which each man who had money, was made to supply before leaving port. This purifying took place every morning before breakfast, within twenty degrees, North and South, of the Equator, which the men seemed to enjoy very much, and producing a glow of warmth after coming out of the bath. Also to keeping the prisons clean, dry, and well ventilated, fumigation, aspertion with Chlorid of lime solution *[calcium hypochlorite, a disinfectant]*, using the swing stoves, whenever any dampness appeared between decks. The Bedding taken on deck, aired and well shaken, three times a week.

The bottom boards of the bed places taken up daily, and kept, for several hours to admit air and purification. As soon as we got well clear of the Land every man's Irons were taken off, the prison doors thrown open from Six AM until they were mustered below at night. Keeping the Sentrys always on the alert, with one half the Guard always on deck. Frequently remonstrating on the advantage of good conduct, and to put an immediate check upon those who might attempt to shew a bad example.

The prisoners were made to take exercise on deck when the weather would admit, in the mornings, and evenings, and to enter into amusing games. I had the fore and main hatch way Gratings put on, the distance round the long boat being thirty yards, and as 1760 yards is a mile, going round 58 times gave each man a mile exercise, one third going round at a time; the Band playing on the top of the long boat, and although our Music was not so good as on my former voyage still it was sufficient to enliven them, and cause them to go at a double quick pace. Dancing was kept up for several hours in the evenings which exercise I consider highly conducive to health on board a Convict Ship, as in a small space exercise can be taken by a great many at the same time.

The School which was early formed was attended by a great many, and considerable progress made. Divine Service every sunday on deck when the weather would admit, and in the Prison and Hospital on all other occasions. Prisoners in ill health were read to separately and Exhorted to Prayer, the scripture expounded to them, such portions being selected as seemed most appropriate and calculated to make a deep impression, and I have reason to believe that in some it was productive of good effect.

Admiral Hawker contributed largely to our stock of religious books, not on this occasion alone, but on the two former; indeed I believe he sends a number of religious books on board all the Convict Ships for which I hope he will have his reward.

I beg leave to mention that it was my intention to have gone to the Cape, and gave the Master of the Ship directions to steer for that port, which he did, but the wind coming from the N:E: and being in Longitude 16.44 it was thought more prudent to pursue our course which we did.

STORM AT SEA

On approaching that far distant land New South Wales, our Scorbutic Sick shewed great amendment, I was constantly cheering up those who were low spirited, and telling them that in a few days they would have fresh Beef and vegetables; and that a run on the turf, or terra firma, would soon remove all pains and stiffness from their bones, and I had great hopes that few of them would prove hospital cases. But Alas! my hopes were soon frustrated.

On the 5th of May with a strong breeze from the South E: by E:, dark foggy weather. Thermometer 50 & not having had sights for the Chronometer the day before we stood in to make the land; which proved to be the Rain Head in Bass's straits [*the sea between what are now Victoria and Tasmania*], the weather being dark, foggy with drizzling rain we got close in shore before the land could be seen. The breeze increased to a heavy gale. Being on a Lee shore we required to carry a press of canvas to clear Cape Howe [*south-east tip of Australia, where New South Wales and Victoria now meet*]. The Gale increased with thunder, Lightning and heavy rain. The Topsails were close reefed but the Gusts became so very violent that all three topgallantmasts, sails, &c went close to the Cap's, Split the fore and main topsails to threads, Blew the fore and mainsails from the Yards & not leaving a Yard of canvas to be seen, Ship labouring heavily and shiping green seas over all. Ship hove too under <u>bare poles</u>, the Gale increased to a perfect Hurricane, "which is called here <u>A brick fielder</u>" [*strictly the Brickfielder is a hot, dry, dusty, northerly wind blowing across SE Australia, but it is rapidly followed by a polar south-westerly wind with violent storms*]. The violence of the Sea broke the side scuttles in, and much water made its way into the Prison and Hospital down the Hatchways filling the prison so full that the lower bed places on the larbourd [*larboard/port - left if looking from stern to bows*] side were more than two inches covered with water, all hands in the prison were employed bailing the water out all night. The Sick were got up to wind[w]ard, unfortunately there was no scupper on the larboard side of the deck to allow the water to pass into the hold.

Figure 5.8 A perfect hurricane

About midnight the ship was struck by a heavy sea on the Starboard side, burst in the Scuttles again, <u>and knocked down every standing bed place on that side, fore and aft,</u> making a clean <u>sweep</u> of that side, Carrying the unfortunate Sick to almost a watery grave on the opposite side, with their Kits, Kegs, Tin pots, bags & broken planks, full of nails, some tons of Water must have come down the Hatchways as the sea went nearly as high as the Main Tops of the Ship having broached too. I cannot express the panic and dismay this occurrence caused, as most of them thought they were going to the bottom.

I fortunately was in the Hospital at the time the bed places gave way; when I recovered from <u>my own fright</u> I tried to appease theirs. Got the Sick into the upper bed-places on the Lb^d side; those who had dry beds and shirts were caused to give them to the Sick, which was done with much less grumbling than I expected. The Hurricane continued until 7P.M. of the next day. The pumps were kept constantly going assisted by the Prisoners.

As soon as the Carpenters could be got to work the prison was cleared of all the broken down berths, and a lower tier of bed places erected, the damage done been too great to have them all rebuilt, the prisoners were got in the best order possible under the circumstances. The wet bedding and cloths got on deck, indeed there was not a Bed, blanket, or particle of clothing except what was in the upper bed places on the Lee side that was not saturated, and trodden into the dirt, and for several days after could not be got dry, although hung up on lines &c &c

I know few things more impressive than the sounds caused by the flaping of a wet sail in such a fierce Gale as this, when the sheets are carried away, and the unconfined sail tuging and tearing to get clear of the Yard - The Prince George is a weak ship and constantly leaked in her top sides during half the voyage. The lower bed places in the Hospital were useless from Leaks. This unfortunate circumstance, "with that of our starting," produced such debility that on our arrival at Sydney I was obliged to send twenty seven men to the Hospital in different grades of the Disease.

I beg to mention that George Edward Peacock's conduct throughout the Voyage was most Exemplary and I am happy to say that I was enabled through the intercession of friends to get him the situation of Gate Keeper at his present destination. <u>Especials</u>, not being assigned, he subsequently was employed as a Clerk.

Signed   **Thomas Bell (c) Surgeon RN**

CHAPTER 6

JUSTICE AND REPERCUSSIONS

The sudden, unplanned absence of the family breadwinner would cause grave problems for family members left behind, even in the strongest of families. So how did John Porter's family cope?

THE CONVICT'S WIFE

Ann Porter might have seen her husband again once or twice after 18 October 1836 if she was able to travel the nine miles to Folkingham gaol, but she would have had difficulty visiting him once he had been transferred to Lincoln Castle. There would certainly have been no further opportunity to see him once he had been taken from Lincoln to the prison hulk moored on the Thames in London. Ann was left to raise her four sons alone. Her eldest son, John, had just turned thirteen so he and George, the second eldest, would have been able to earn a little, but the other two were too young. The next few years must have been very difficult for Ann.

Her parents, William and Amy Thimbleby, had lived in Bourne from the time of their marriage in 1796 and all their children had been born there. Both parents were in their late sixties when their son-in-law was convicted and transported. William was still able to work as an agricultural labourer but any help they could offer to Ann and her sons would have been modest. Whether Ann or any of her sons went to live with the Thimblebys is not known. Ann was living in Counthorpe in May 1840 where her third son died. The death certificate reads: 'Charles Porter, male, age 11 years, son of labourer [unnamed]' and the cause of death 'typhus fever' [It is not clear whether this was *typhoid fever*, spread by contaminated food or water, or *typhus*, a different illness spread by rats or lice]. The Revd William Tennant entered this information in the parish burial register. The informant, whose name appears on the death certificate, was Mary Porter, suggesting that Ann was at least receiving some support from her in-laws.

Ann Thimbleby Porter had a sister Mary, who was married to Thomas Farrow, so some support may have been available from the Thimbleby side of the family. However, Farrow died early in 1841, leaving Mary with four young children to raise. When the 1841 census was taken, Mary and her children were living with her parents in Bourne, so it would then have been difficult to accommodate Ann and her family as well.

The 1841 census confirms that Ann and her youngest son, Frederick, had remained in Counthorpe but the older boys, John and George, were away working elsewhere in Lincolnshire at Deeping Fen and Gosberton respectively.

Normally the parish vestry records would reveal the names of persons receiving parish relief, but records for the parish of Castle Bytham no longer exist. Admission records to the Union Workhouse would identify those in the most desperate circumstances, and neither Ann Porter nor any of her children appear during those initial years without the main breadwinner, so they were not forced to enter the Bourne Union Poor House. So it seems Ann managed somehow, probably reliant on family support alone.

Meanwhile, back in Counthorpe life continued with little apparent change for Ann's neighbours. The first four households enumerated in the Hamlet of Counthorpe in the 1841 census can be seen in Fig.6.1. Ann Porter, age 45, and her son Frederick, 5, occupy the first dwelling. Next door is Thomas Robinson, age 25, an agricultural labourer, and his wife Mary (née Mary Alice Spridgen), whose age is stated as 30 but she was 38 years old by then. Also in the Robinson household are two children from Mary Alice's first marriage, a son Thomas age 10 and daughter Sarah 7, and a son and a daughter of Thomas born after her second marriage. The next house contains George Hodson and his wife Mary, both 50, and their son George, 25. Both father and son were agricultural

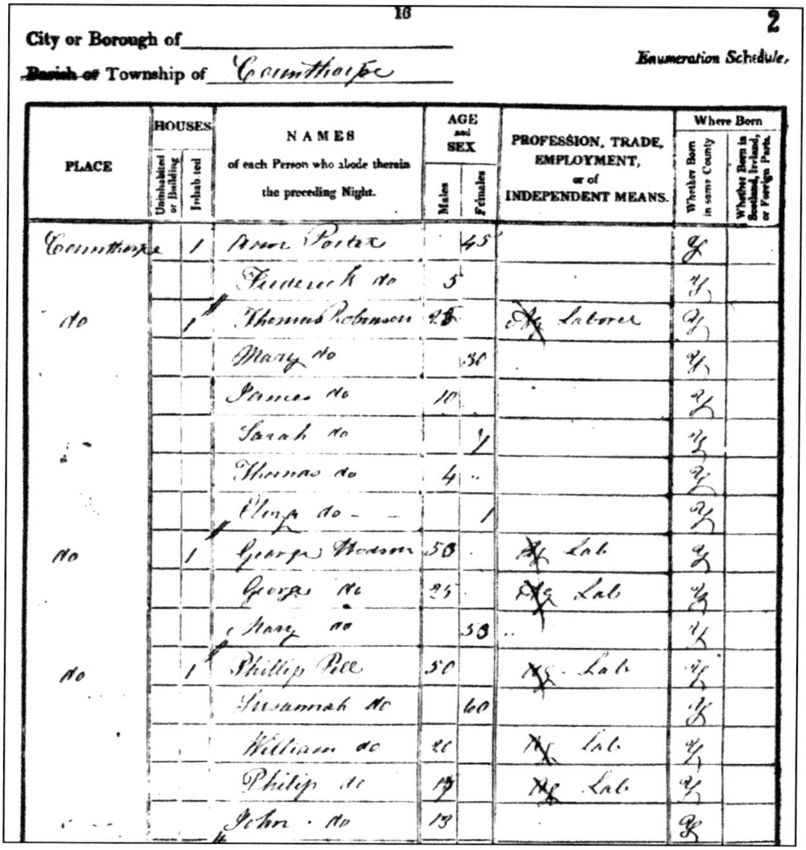

PLACE	HOUSES: Uninhabited or Building	HOUSES: Inhabited	NAMES of each Person who abode therein the preceding Night.	AGE and SEX: Males	AGE and SEX: Females	PROFESSION, TRADE, EMPLOYMENT, or of INDEPENDENT MEANS.	Where Born: Whether Born in same County	Where Born: Whether Born in Scotland, Ireland, or Foreign Parts.
Counthorpe		1	Ann Porter		45		Y	
			Frederick do	5			Y	
do		1	Thomas Robinson	25		Ag Laborer	Y	
			Mary do		30		Y	
			James do	10			Y	
			Sarah do		7		Y	
			Thomas do	4			Y	
			Eliza do		1		Y	
do		1	George [illegible]	50		Ag Lab	Y	
			George do	25		Ag Lab	Y	
			Mary do		55		Y	
do		1	Phillip Pell	50		Ag Lab	Y	
			Susannah do		60		Y	
			William do	20		Ag Lab	Y	
			Philip do	15		Ag Lab	Y	
			John do	13			Y	

Figure 6.1 Ann Porter and her neighbours in the 1841 census of Counthorpe

labourers. So five years after the trial, Ann's nearest neighbours were the same two women whose testimony helped William Tennant secure his conviction and condemn Ann to single parenthood.

The fourth house lists another agricultural labourer, Philip Pell, 50, his three sons and Suzanna his wife, who died the following year. On 5 December 1843, seven years after her husband's conviction, Ann Porter, described as a widow, married Philip Pell in the Baptist church in Bourne. Since a period of seven years had elapsed since Ann's first husband had been transported, her re-marriage did not count as bigamy. In effect, Ann had also received a sentence: seven years as a single parent.

Philip Pell had been married twice previously and his three sons still living at home were all unmarried agricultural labourers in their late teens or early twenties when Philip married Ann. All the males of working age in Counthorpe were still agricultural labourers, with one or two exceptions who had become tenant farmers. The owners of the land lived elsewhere. Later in the 1840s, employment opportunities began to change in this area. The 1851 census shows Philip, Ann and two of Philip's sons, together with four other people living in the Pell household in Counthorpe. The strangers were all involved in building the railroad; almost all the dwellings in Counthorpe were providing lodgings for railroad construction workers at that time.

Figure 6.2 Recent photograph of the railroad at Counthorpe

Philip Pell died in February 1861 and Ann appeared in that year's census as a widow, living in Counthorpe with two of Philip's sons. Ten years later Ann was still living in Counthorpe with one stepson, but by now she was blind. Her own son Frederick lived nearby, but he had experienced one family tragedy after another. Four of his children had died at very young ages during the 1860s and early 1870s, and his wife's death in April 1875 must have limited the care he could provide for his geriatric mother. Philip's sons, however, cared for their stepmother in the later stages of her life, but eventually Ann was admitted to the workhouse a few months before her death.

Bourne Poor Law Union was formed in 1835 and its operation was overseen by an elected Board of Guardians representing its constituent parishes. The new workhouse was built in 1836-7 at the end of Union Road (now called St Peter's Road) on the west side of Bourne, and was designed to accommodate 300 inmates. Union Workhouses were deliberately intended to be mean, unpleasant, miserable places, to deter people from choosing to be admitted.

Ann Thimbleby Porter Pell died in the Bourne Union Workhouse on 15 December 1876 and three days later was buried in the graveyard of the parish church of Castle Bytham. If any gravestone marking her burial site was ever erected, it has long since disappeared.

THE CONVICT'S PARENTS

Two weeks after John Porter first set foot in New South Wales, his father, John Porter (1763-1837) was dead. His death, in May 1837, occurred just before the start of civil registration of births, marriages and deaths in England, so the cause of his death is not recorded. The Witham on the Hill parish records confirm that he was still living in Lound and give his age as seventy-six, though he may have been a year or two younger. Nevertheless, by reaching his mid-seventies John had outlived the normal lifespan for an early nineteenth-century Englishman. His son's trial, conviction and exile doubtless meant that the final few months of his life were not his happiest.

Charlotte Porter, the convict's mother, lived on in Lound for a further eighteen months, then died of a fever on 19 November 1838. Whether she harboured regrets that she allowed William Tennant to interview her about the type of meat she gave her son on Lound Feast Day in 1836 or whether she ever knew that Tennant used her gift of beef to help gain his conviction, we shall never know.

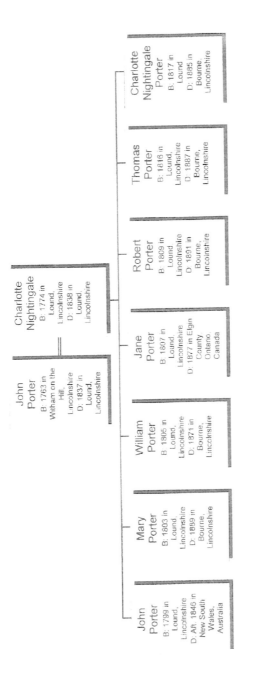

Figure 6.3 The convict's parents and siblings

THE CONVICT'S SIBLINGS

Charlotte Porter's death registration certificate names Mary Fisher as the informant and states that she was present at the death. Mary Fisher was the eldest surviving daughter of John and Charlotte Porter. She and her husband, John Fisher, had lived in Lound until the mid-1830s, but had recently moved to the market town of Bourne, two miles north-east of Lound, at the time of her mother's death.

Mary Fisher appears to have facilitated the first wave of Porter migrations by assisting her younger brothers to leave the hamlet in which they were born and relocate to the nearest market town, Bourne. So Feast Day in Lound in 1836 would have been the last time the Porter family were together. Within a few months, both parents died and all the children moved away. Seven of their ten children had reached adulthood; the others were Charlotte (1801-12), Charlotte (b./d.1814), and Richard (1814-16).

By the June 1841 census all the children of John Porter (1763-1837) and his wife Charlotte had left Lound. Their sons, William and Robert, and their daughters, Mary and Charlotte Nightingale Porter, had all married and were now living in Bourne. Their youngest son Thomas was still unmarried in 1841 but he too was living in Bourne in the home of his sister Mary Fisher. Another sister, Jane, was married and living in Quadring, twelve miles north-east of Bourne. Whether the stigma of a convicted felon in the family prompted any of the convict's siblings to leave Lound is difficult to judge. What can be shown is that the population decline of Lound between 1831 and 1841 is more or less accounted for by the exodus of the children and grand-children of John and Charlotte Porter during this decade. A more likely reason for the wholesale departure of the Porter family from Lound to Bourne was one of simple economics.

The economy of Lound was based entirely on agriculture, an unpredictable and risky industry. Although Bourne was a small market town, the economy was more diversified. Bourne's shopkeepers and tradesmen offered alternative employment opportunities. The Porters and thousands of other families like them were joining the huge migration that was already in full swing from rural to urban Britain. The ending in 1834 of the need for a Settlement Certificate when moving to another parish made such moves easier, further increasing the mobility of the labour force.

The *Lewis Topgraphical Dictionary of England*, 1831, describes Bourne as 'a market town containing 2,242 inhabitants ... 36 miles (S) from Lincoln, and 97 (N) from London'. The discovery of Roman coins and tesselated pavements suggests it may once have been a place of some importance. In the ninth century, Marcot, the Saxon lord of Bourne, with a few of his own vassals and a detachment from Croyland Abbey, defeated a party of invading Danes. Prior to the time of Edward the Confessor, a castle was built, of which only the trenches and mounds are now discernible. In the seventeenth century, Bourne was twice nearly destroyed by fire. 'The town, consisting principally of one very long street, the houses in which are in general modern and well built, is pleasantly situated, and plentifully supplied with excellent water. The trade is chiefly in leather and wool; for the former there are several extensive tan-yards. A navigable canal as been constructed from this town to Spalding and Boston, by which means it is supplied with coal, timber and other commodities.'

THE CONVICT

Records of convicts taken to New South Wales are generally good and several relating to John Porter can be found in both Britain and Australia. There is information about him in the trial records, for time spent on the hulk *Justitia*, for the voyage to NSW, and from the penal colony. The policy in force when John Porter arrived was to assign well-behaved prisoners to settlers. A Convict Muster Roll taken shortly after his arrival in NSW shows that he was initially assigned to a Master, John King, in the Murray District. In 1837 this district covered a huge territory on both sides of the Murray River, much of it still unexplored by Europeans. The Murray River now forms part of the boundary separating the State of New South Wales from the State of Victoria, but when John Porter was there Victoria had not yet been granted statehood so the whole area was still part of New South Wales.

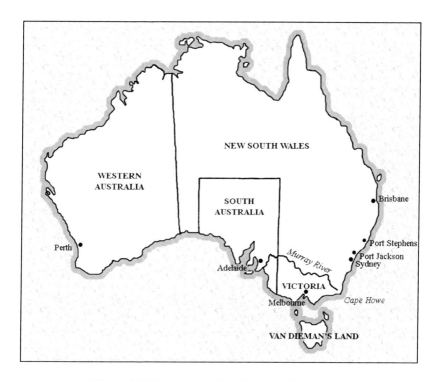

Figure 6.4 Map of Australia showing NSW in 1851

Britain's need for penal colonies went beyond the desire simply to get rid of convicted felons; there were attractive commercial opportunities to be exploited, even in penal colonies where large numbers of convicts could provide inexpensive labour.

One example was the Australian Agricultural Company (AA Company), established in 1824 by an Act of Parliament in Britain. The principal shareholders were among the most prominent people in Britain, including the Attorney-General (the person responsible for determining sentencing policy in the courts), the Solicitor-General of England, two dozen Members of Parliament, the Governor and several Directors of the

Bank of England, and the Chairman and some Directors of the British East India Company. The AA Company's main objective was to improve flocks of merino sheep in New South Wales and then export them back to Britain. The initial area selected for operations under the founding charter amounted to nearly half a million acres and extended from Port Stephens, embracing the Karuah Valley and the Gloucester Flats, to the Manning River, including most of the northern shore of Port Stephens.

Figure 6.5 The Founding of Australia, 1788
Painting by Algernon Talmage RA
Image courtesy of **Mitchell Library, State Library of NSW**

The AA Company needed large numbers of convict labourers to operate and administered notoriously harsh treatment on them. Floggings were so frequent that the Company employed a permanent flagellator. Many convicts tried to escape, but soldiers were stationed nearby, at what is now known as Soldier's Point near Port Stephens, to apprehend and return those who tried to escape.

Convicts assigned to Port Stephens went with dread. Many attempted to escape rather than face the likelihood of being worked, starved or flogged to death in captivity. Overseers drove the convicts without mercy, often beating them to the ground with clubs and then beating them to their feet again. It was common for convicts to work up to twenty hours a day, six days a week, often in leg-irons. Their diet was limited to the most basic foods, such as boiled maize and salted beef, with little variety. Those found guilty of any offence were stripped, lashed to a whipping triangle, and flogged by a Ticket of Leave convict who was himself under threat of a whipping if he was seen to go lightly with the lash. Fifty lashes was a common sentence for even trivial wrongdoings. Whippings were alway held on a Sunday so that all convicts could witness the punishment.

John Porter appears in the Australian convict records again in 1846 when his Ticket of Leave was granted. Convicts serving a seven-year term, with good conduct, could expect to receive a Ticket of Leave after four or five years; those serving a fourteen-year term after six to eight years, while those sentenced to life could get their ticket after ten to twelve years. A Ticket of Leave was similar to a parole but, since Porter had received a sentence of life, he was not eligible to apply for a pardon.

Convicts could apply to marry, usually after seven years, but no record of an application by John Porter has been found. When a person has disappeared without trace, seven years is the usual period to elapse before

Figure 6.6 A.A. Co Button

a surviving spouse can legitimately remarry. This was taken to apply to transported convicts too.

John Porter must have maintained good conduct because his Ticket of Leave was granted earlier than for most 'lifers'. The absence, however, of an application to marry, along with his good conduct, means that there are fewer records relating to him after 1846. This makes him harder to trace.

Once his Ticket of Leave had been granted, John Porter, then aged forty-seven, was free to seek employment or go into business, but he was required to remain within a defined area and there were reporting conditions.

There were at least eleven other men with the name John Porter transported from Britain to New South Wales in the early nineteenth century, making the search to find ours more challenging. Like many other ex-convicts at this time, once he had his Ticket of Leave, the John Porter who arrived on the *Prince George* in 1837 simply disappeared. There were better places to live than Port Stephens.

Government Gazette.

FRIDAY, JUNE 19, 1846.

His Excellency the Governor has been pleased to make the following appointments in the department of Customs, viz. :—Charles Bolton, Esq., to be Sub-collector of Customs and Warehouse-keeper at Newcastle; Thomas James Blair, Esq., to be Landing Waiter at the same place.

TICKETS OF LEAVE.

The undermentioned prisoners of the crown have obtained tickets of leave since the last day of publication :—

Scone—Cheshire Thomas, Waterloo 5; Johnstone Michael, Westmoreland.

Invermein—Morgan Phillip, Asia 11.

Merton—Parr John, Lloyds 2.

Muswell Brook—Pio Juan Blafane, Theresa.

Port Stephens—Porter John, Prince George.

Dungog—Dart Edward, Portsea.

Maitland—Keane John, Westmoreland; Wood William, Barrosa.

Newcastle—Green William, John Barry 4.

Patrick's Plains—Thompson Joseph, Norfolk.

The tickets of leave of the undermentioned prisoners of the crown have been cancelled for the reasons stated opposite their respective names :—

Thomas Tool, Blenheim, larceny; Cassilis. Henry Andrews, Norfolk, prevarication in giving evidence; Stroud.

Figure 6.7 Excerpt from *Maitland Mercury* 24 June 1846, reporting the *Government Gazette* announcement a few days earlier

CHAPTER 7

MIGRATION - PART OF THE HUMAN STORY

As John Porter spent day after day bobbing up and down with the waves, enduring the lengthy voyage to Australia, he may have wondered if any of his family had travelled such distances or experienced such a migration before.

People living in nineteenth-century England might have some idea of their origins from oral information handed down from earlier generations. Most uneducated people, however, would have little idea of when their ancestors came to Britain or where from. People whose surname ended with -by, like John Porter's wife Ann Thimbleby, were likely to be of Norse origin, but it was a thousand years since the Vikings or Norsemen had ruled that part of Britain.

John Porter might have been aware of some of Britain's more recent history, mainly because of the migrations of some of his neighbours. People in Witham on the Hill would have been aware that prominent members of the Johnson family had migrated to America in the seventeenth century and others had followed.

Over four centuries the British had planted colonies all over the world. These colonies required sufficient settlers to populate them quickly enough to maintain their sustainability. From lessons learned from Britain's difficulties in sustaining her initial attempt to plant a colony at Jamestown in Virginia in 1607, it became clear that many migrants were needed at the outset. For example, the new colonies that were established in Ireland in the early seventeenth century were planted with settlers more quickly. But even then, of the four colonies planted in Ireland, only one, the plantation in Ulster, managed to survive.

John Porter's mother-in-law, Amy Thimbleby, might have told him of the migration experiences of her father's Huguenot ancestors. The Norse had come to Britain as conquerors, but the Huguenots came as refugees seeking asylum from religious persecution in mainland Europe.

Figure 7.1 Le Massacre de la St Barthélemy, 1572-1584 by François Dubois
Image courtesy of J.-C. Ducret, Musée Cantonal des Beaux-Arts, Lausanne

EARLY MIGRANTS TO BRITAIN

Migration has been part of the human story from its beginning. One migration, for which the main evidence is linguistic, is the way that Celts once covered much of Europe, certainly the north from central Europe west. More advanced technology for both warfare and agriculture enabled them to survive and spread, until they in turn were pushed back to the western fringes of the continent by ever more advanced peoples.

The first mass migrants into Lincolnshire were probably Celts, followed later by Romans. Angles and Saxons began to flow in during the sixth and seventh centuries. Then in 735 came Norse raiding parties from what are now Denmark and Norway. These early Viking raiders did not settle. In AD 865 large numbers of Danes landed in East Anglia with the intention of staying. Their army marched north, invaded Northumbria, then descended again on East Anglia in 869-870, defeating the Anglo-Saxon kingdom there.

While these were a fairly diverse set of Norse tribes and clans, speaking a variety of different although related languages, they had much in common. Their social, tribal and political structures were more or less similar and they shared common religious beliefs. As they migrated out of their homelands their ethnic identity became confused. The Norse emigrants were prepared to adopt the language, culture and even religion of the areas where they settled. The clan structure that characterised their life was often given up during a single generation as they quickly adapted to the existing societies in their new lands.

The territory that the Norse conquered was immense. They settled in northern England, northern France, Scotland, the Orkneys, Ireland, Iceland, Greenland and even reached as far west as North America and east to Russia and Byzantium, always adjusting to the local culture. Only those Norse settlers who went to Iceland held on to their traditional ways of life and culture, because they found there no indigenous population.

By the early tenth century the English (descended from Anglo-Saxons) had managed to regain East Anglia and then Lincolnshire and other nearby counties. A century later the Danes raided East Anglia again and by 1016 defeated the English. Then in 1066 the Normans arrived, themselves descended from Norse invaders in France. All these invaders contributed to the cultural and, especially, the linguistic mix of Britain.

Arab people from Tyre also spread out across North Africa and eventually pushed northward into Spain, bringing with them their advanced Islamic culture. The migrations of the Arabs and the Celts took centuries to develop. There are countless more examples of mankind packing up home in one place and settling in another. The reasons why people migrate are also so numerous and varied that a few examples only can be contained in a book such as this.

THE HUGUENOTS

An important migration into Britain began in the late sixteenth century when groups of French-speaking Protestants began to flee from religious persecution in France and the Low Countries. Their troubles escalated in 1572 when Roman Catholic mob violence turned on them. An estimated 2,000 Huguenots were killed in Paris, including many of their wealthiest and most prominent leaders. A further 3,000 Huguenots perished in the French countryside. This slaughter marked the turning point in the French Wars of Religion and, having lost so many of their leaders, the Huguenots were defenceless against continuing persecution. Gradually they began to migrate.

Many were Walloons from Northern France and what is now Belgium. They scattered widely to England, Ireland, Russia and the new British colonies in America. In England Huguenots settled especially in Canterbury, London, and Sandtoft in Lincolnshire, as well as around Honiton, where they established the lace industry.

In the early seventeenth century the colony at Sandtoft consisted of about 200 French and Walloon families. They soon became engaged in the largest civil engineering project in Europe at the time, a scheme to reclaim land from the fens in Lincolnshire and Cambridgeshire. The project was led by the Dutch drainage engineer, Cornelius Vermuyden, and his work force was heavily supplemented by these new migrants already experienced in ditching and embanking in the Low Countries (the Netherlands and Belgium).

Some of the Huguenot newcomers migrated purely for economic reasons. The indigenous population began to resent these 'strangers' and from 1642 attacked the newcomers in Sandtoft, together with their earthworks, reflooding some parts of the fens. The settlers began to move to a second colony at Thorney, near Peterborough, and by 1650 all the 'strangers' had left Sandtoft. The colony at Thorney was more successful and draining of the fens continued. The map below shows the significance of this project which converted marshland to fertile agricultural land in counties that border the large indentation on the east coast of England known as 'The Wash'.

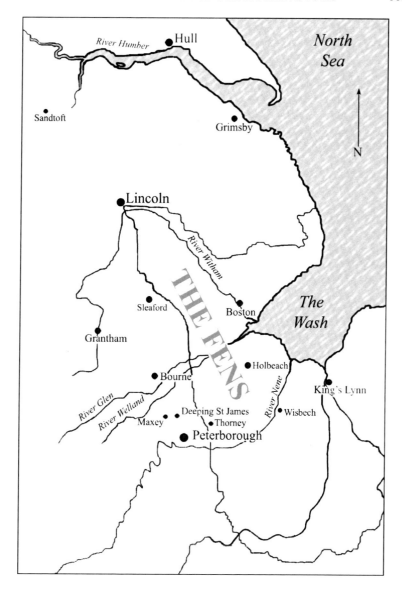

Figure 7.2 The Fens
The Fens lie around the Wash in four counties, Lincolnshire,
Cambridgeshire, Norfolk and a small area of Suffolk

The Wash is an inlet of the North Sea, twenty miles long and fifteen wide, between Lincolnshire and Norfolk on the east coast of England. It receives the Witham, Welland, Nene and Ouse rivers. It is mostly shallow with sandbars and low, marshy shores. Dredged ship channels lead to King's Lynn and Boston.

John Porter's mother-in-law, Amy Merilion Thimbleby, was of Huguenot descent. Amy's name appears in some records as Amey and there are over twenty variations in the spelling of her surname, the most common of which are Merilion, Merillion, and Morillion. The arrival of the Huguenots in Lincolnshire made a considerable impact on the topography of the region and the local population.

Settlement Certificate
Isle of Ely   To Wit

To the Churchwardens and Overseers of the Poor
Of the Parish of Deeping St James in the County of Lincoln

We whose Names are hereunto subscribed Churchwardens and Overseer of the Poor of the Parish of Thorney in the Isle of Ely in the county of Cambridge Do hereby own and acknowledge Isaac Merillion, Hannah his wife, Zachariah and Abraham their children, to be inhabitants legally settled in our Parish of Thorney aforesaid: And if they become chargeable do promise to receive and provide for them as our Poor unless they gain a legal settlement elsewhere. In witness whereof we the said Churchwardens and Overseer have hereunto respectively set our hands and Seals this 9th day of June 1748.

Attested by: Henry Haddon   Church Warden
**   Alfd. Milson   Seal Affixed**
Nicholas Savage   Overseer of the Poor
**   Will Adey   Seal Affixed**

Figure 7.3 Transcript of Settlement Certificate of
Amy Merilion Thimbleby's grandparents

There were people surnamed Merlion in the early settlement at Sandtoft, but it is more likely that Amy Merilion's ancestors were attracted to Thorney directly from Canterbury where there were a considerable number so named. Amy's father, Zachariah Merilion, was born in Thorney, Cambridgeshire, in 1737. A Settlement Deed dated 1748 survives, granting his parents, Isaac and Hannah Merilion, and their two sons the right to reside in the parish of Deeping St James. The original can be found in the Lincolnshire Archives. A transcription appears opposite.

The Settlement Act 1662

One of the factors that inhibited internal migration within Britain between the seventeenth and nineteenth centuries was legislation entitled *An Act for the Better Relief of the Poor of this Kingdom*, which became known as the Settlement Act. Its purpose was to establish the parish in which each person belonged (where they were *settled*) and thereby to clarify which parish was responsible should that person need assistance or become a financial burden on the parish. This was the first time in British history when a document proving a person's place of domicile came into use and these were called Settlement Certificates.

To gain settlement in a parish a person had to meet one of these conditions:

- been born in the parish
- lived there for three years
- married into the parish
- gained poor relief in the parish previously
- entered into a seven-year apprenticeship with a settled resident, or
- been in continuous employment there for at least a year (but to prevent this, labourers were often hired for a period of 364 days rather than a full year, which is how the parish of Witham on the Hill was able to rid itself of John Porter in 1820).

This Act allowed a parish to send newcomers back to the parishes they had previously inhabited if the local justices thought them likely to become a financial burden on the new parish. Exemption was given if the new arrival was able to rent a property costing at least £10 a year, but that was well beyond the means of the typical agricultural labourer.

A child's settlement at birth was taken to be that of his father. At marriage, a woman took on the same settlement as her husband. Illegitimate children were granted settlement in the place where they were born, and this sometimes led to parish overseers trying to get rid of a unmarried pregnant woman before the birth, perhaps by transporting her to another parish just before the baby was due, or by paying a man from another parish to marry her. A boy might be apprenticed from as young as seven, and would then take the same settlement as his master.

From 1662 onwards, if a man moved away from his settled parish, he had to obtain his Settlement Certificate, which guaranteed that his home parish would pay for his 'removal' costs back home if he fell on hard times and needed poor relief. Parishes were often unwilling to issue such certificates. This encouraged people to stay where they were, knowing that in emergency they would be entitled to their parish's poor rate.

The Settlement Act benefited the owners of large estates as they controlled the supply of available housing in the parish. Some landowners demolished empty housing in order to reduce the population of their lands and prevent people from returning. It was also common to recruit labourers from neighbouring parishes so that, when their employment was terminated, the parish could avoid poor relief if they failed to find fresh work quickly. Much agricultural labour is seasonal. Magistrates had the power to order parishes to grant poor relief but magistrates were often landowners unlikely to make relief orders that would increase the poor rates. The financial burden of poor rates would fall more heavily on those with larger houses and more money.

The Settlement Act was replaced when the Poor Law Amendment Act of 1834 came into force, introducing the Union Workhouse. From the mid-1830s workhouses were established to accommodate the destitute from groups of parishes (unions). The incentive for a parish to avoid responsibility for another parish's poor and needy began to disappear. Living conditions in these new, larger workhouses were made deliberately dire to deter people from entering and many suffered as a result. The Poor Law Amendment Act was therefore both a carrot and a stick to migration. This Act made internal migration much easier because Settlement Certificates were no longer required, while the poor and needy were forced through circumstances and starvation to seek work wherever it could be found. The newly developing industrial system welcomed these changes because they drove workers willing to accept low wages to factory towns.

Nineteenth-Century Migration from Britain

In early nineteenth century Britain many forces were at work putting pressure upon and uprooting the population. Economic, social and political changes had been causing upheaval and reforms were slow to materialise. The prolonged recession had created chronic unemployment, particularly in the south of England, where there was a surplus of agricultural labourers. Civil disobedience, some violent, had been attempted in several English counties and Scotland. Resistance had been met with draconian measures.

Some of the more enlightened parishes and more benevolent landowners recognised both the need and the economic benefit of assisting their unemployed to seek new opportunities for themselves through migration. All sorts of migration schemes were conceived, most involving just a few individuals or families, but larger schemes were also attempted. One well documented example began in West Sussex and became known as the Petworth Project.

In the 1830s, Thomas Sockett, the rector of Petworth, a parish in Sussex, organised the emigration of about 1,800 men, women and children to Upper Canada. This regional scheme involved men, who were mainly agricultural labourers struggling to find employment, a number of English parishes and some landowners wishing to dispose of their surplus labour.

The migrants were men and their families who came from several different counties in southern England. They were transported on ships chartered specifically for the scheme and went initially to York (which changed its name to Toronto in 1834). The Government of Upper Canada provided some advice and assistance upon their arrival and the migrants were then settled in different places in what is now south western Ontario. Some travelled as far west as Port Stanley, settling in the nearby Townships of Yarmouth, Southwold, Adelaide and Mosa.

The Petworth migration scheme (1832-37) was financed by George O'Brien Wyndham, the third Earl of Egremont, with support from about 100 English parishes and many landowners. This scheme was one of many where landowners and English parishes collaborated on migration schemes designed to reduce England's over-abundance of agricultural labourers in the 1830s. This proved to be one of the more successful schemes of the 1830s. With assistance before leaving, during travel and upon arrival, migrants were given a better chance of adjusting happily to their new environment. Migrants were also settled in groups so neighbours whom they already knew could help in times of difficulty. But more important still, land was available in Upper Canada to purchase at a cost that was affordable, so almost all could aspire to own a farm of their own. [For those wishing to know more about this project, the book *Assisting Emigration to Upper Canada: The Petworth Project, 1832-1837* by Wendy Cameron and Mary McDougall Maude is recommended.]

Three sons of the convict, John Porter, all decided to migrate in search of a better life, though these were migrations of choice unlike their father's forced migration. Case studies of each form part of the next chapters.

Figure 7.4 (on page 119) Migration Poster, 1888
Crown Copyright. The National Archives of Scotland AAA00476
Image courtesy of Scotlandimages.com

POSTER.

1st October, 1888.

Office Open—
Every week day but Saturday 10.30 a.m. to 6.30 p.m.
Saturday 10.30 a.m. to 2 p.m. only.

Note.—This office has been established under the supervision of the Colonial Office for the purpose of supplying intending emigrants with useful and trustworthy information respecting emigration to the British Colonies. The information issued to the public is mainly obtained from the various Colonial Governments and their representatives in this country. No pains are spared to make the information as accurate as possible, but the committee of management cannot undertake to hold themselves responsible for the absolute correctness of every detail.

GENERAL INFORMATION
FOR INTENDING
EMIGRANTS
TO
CANADA, THE AUSTRALASIAN AND SOUTH AFRICAN COLONIES.

LENGTH AND COST OF PASSAGE.

The Time ordinarily taken on the voyage, and the lowest rate of unassisted passages to the above Colonies, are as follows:—

	BY STEAMER.		BY SAILING VESSEL.	
	Average Time.	Lowest Fare. (Liable to change) £ s. d.	Average Time.	Lowest Fare. (Liable to change) £ s. d.
CANADA	9 10 days	4 0 0		
NEW SOUTH WALES	45 52 ,,	14 14 0	About 3 months	13 13 0
VICTORIA	42 49 ,,	14 14 0	Nearly 3 months	13 13 0
SOUTH AUSTRALIA	40 46 ,,	14 14 0	3 months	12 12 0
QUEENSLAND	55 ,,	15 15 0	About 3 months	15 3 0
WESTERN AUSTRALIA	35 40 ,,	16 16 0	3 months	14 14 0
TASMANIA	40 50 ,,	14 14 0	,, 3 months	14 12 0
NEW ZEALAND	45 ,,	16 16 0	,, 3 months	13 13 0
CAPE	20 ,,	15 15 0		
NATAL	26 28 ,,	18 18 0		

PASSAGES.

1. FREE PASSAGES.—QUEENSLAND.—To selected unmarried Agricultural Labourers and single Female Domestic Servants (apply to the Agent General). No Free Passages to any other Colony.

2. ASSISTED PASSAGES.—WESTERN AUSTRALIA.—£10 is allowed to Farmers, Agriculturists, and others likely to be useful in country districts; but a deposit of not less than £100 (to be refunded on arrival in the Colony) is as a rule required before any assistance is given.

QUEENSLAND.—Assisted passages are given to unmarried labourers connected with the land, as Ploughmen, Gardeners, &c., and to Female Servants, at the following rates:—*Males*, 12 to 40, £5; 40 to 55, £12. *Females*, 12 to 40, £4; and 40 to 55, £12.

No Assisted Passages are given at the present time to CANADA, NEW SOUTH WALES, VICTORIA, SOUTH AUSTRALIA, TASMANIA, NEW ZEALAND, The CAPE or NATAL; but in the case of QUEENSLAND and the CAPE passages at lower rates are given, under special conditions, to Labourers engaged here by employers in those Colonies.

In the case of QUEENSLAND, Land Order Warrants to the value of £20 are given under certain conditions to persons paying their own passage direct to the Colony.

3. NOMINATED PASSAGES.—QUEENSLAND, WESTERN AUSTRALIA, and NATAL.—Residents in these Colonies can, under certain specified conditions, nominate their friends for Free Passages on making payments in the Colony as under:—

QUEENSLAND.—Males, 1 to 12 years of age, £2; 12 to 40, £4; 40 to 55, £8; Females, 1 to 12, £1; 12 to 40, £2; 40 to 55, £8. Confined to Agricultural and other Labourers connected with the land, and Female Domestic Servants.

WESTERN AUSTRALIA.—On payment of £7 to a limited number of Nominees, approved by the Crown Agents for the Colonies.

NATAL.—£12 per adult.

No Nominated Passages are at present given to CANADA, NEW SOUTH WALES, VICTORIA, SOUTH AUSTRALIA, TASMANIA, NEW ZEALAND, or THE CAPE.

ARRANGEMENTS ON LANDING.

CANADA.—Depôts for emigrants are provided at the ports of Quebec and Halifax and the other principal towns in the Dominion.

NEW SOUTH WALES.—Apply to Mr. G. F. Wise, Immigration Agent, Hyde Park, Sydney.

QUEENSLAND.—There are Depôts at the principal ports and in various parts of the Colony, in which Government assisted emigrants are received free of charge for a few days after arrival.

WESTERN AUSTRALIA.—There is a Labour Registry Office at Perth where Emigrants should apply, but no Government Depôt for the reception of Emigrants is now open.

NEW ZEALAND.—There are Depôts at most of the principal ports for the reception of emigrants.

There are no Government Depôts in VICTORIA, SOUTH AUSTRALIA, TASMANIA, THE CAPE, or NATAL; but there are private agencies in some of these; and the other Colonies, particulars of which are given in the Circulars.

BEST TIME FOR ARRIVING.

CANADA.—April to middle of July—not the Winter months.
NEW SOUTH WALES.—Any month—September to November for preference.
VICTORIA.—Ditto.
SOUTH AUSTRALIA.—May to October.
QUEENSLAND.—April to October inclusive.
WESTERN AUSTRALIA.—September to November.
TASMANIA.—Any month—September to November for preference.
NEW ZEALAND.—September to January inclusive.
CAPE.—Any month—August for preference.
NATAL.—Any month—August for preference.

PRESENT DEMAND FOR LABOUR.

FARMERS WITH CAPITAL.—A demand in all the Colonies.
FARM LABOURERS.—A demand for good men in CANADA, NEW SOUTH WALES, VICTORIA, QUEENSLAND, TASMANIA, and some parts of NEW ZEALAND.
MECHANICS AND GENERAL LABOURERS.—Some demand in MELBOURNE, especially for men connected with the building trades. Little or no demand in any other Colony.
FEMALE DOMESTIC SERVANTS.—A good demand in most districts of Canada and the Australasian Colonies, and a slight one at The Cape.

Particulars as to the state of the Labour Market in the various Colonies from time to time will be given in subsequent editions of this Poster.

NAMES AND ADDRESSES OF COLONIAL REPRESENTATIVES IN ENGLAND.

CANADA.—High Commissioner, 9, Victoria Chambers, Victoria Street, Westminster, S.W.
NEW SOUTH WALES.—Agent General, 5, Westminster Chambers, Victoria Street, S.W.
VICTORIA.—Agent General, 8, Victoria Chambers, Victoria Street, S.W.
SOUTH AUSTRALIA.—Agent General, 8, Victoria Chambers, Victoria Street, S.W.
QUEENSLAND.—Agent General, 1, Westminster Chambers, Victoria Street, S.W.
WESTERN AUSTRALIA.—The Crown Agents for the Colonies, Downing Street, S.W.
NEW ZEALAND.—Agent General, 7, Westminster Chambers, Victoria Street, S.W.
TASMANIA.—Agent General, 3, Westminster Chambers, Victoria Street, S.W.
CAPE.—Agent General, 7, Albert Mansions, Victoria Street, S.W.
NATAL.—Emigration Agent for Natal, 21, Finsbury Circus, E.C.

Further information can be obtained by writing or personally applying to the Chief Clerk at this office, 31, Broadway, Westminster, S.W., from whom the CIRCULARS issued by the Committee of Management respecting the separate Colonies can be obtained gratis, and the new HANDBOOKS, with Maps and fuller information, at the price of 1d. post free for each Colony.

Printed for Her Majesty's Stationery Office by W. P. GRIFFITH & SONS, LD., Prujean Square, Old Bailey, London, E.C.

[480] 1080 [M 12]

CHAPTER 8

MIGRATION TO CANADA WEST

High numbers of migrants went from the British Isles to Canada in the nineteenth century. The process began slowly but, following the War of 1812, Britain finally awoke to the need to settle this important colony with loyal emigrants, before it could be overrun by the expanding republic on Canada's southern border. Among the many who were persuaded to cross the Atlantic in search of a better life in Canada were the three sons of John Porter, the convict whose later years were spent in Australia. The southern part of Ontario was known as Upper Canada 1791-1841 and Canada West 1841-1867, when it became Ontario.

Migration from Europe to North America began about 1585 but it was not until 1607 that the first successful settlement was established at Jamestown in Virginia. Emigrants, many of whom were indentured servants, went to work for owners of tobacco plantations. Although many perished early on, the colony itself managed to survive. Other colonies followed, including one at Plymouth (in today's Massachusetts, USA), when Puritans fleeing religious persecution in Europe arrived on the *Mayflower* in 1620.

Some of the American colonies were used as penal colonies by the British and thousands of men, women and children from all parts of the British Isles were transported to them during the seventeenth and eighteenth centuries. Transportation of convicts to America ended with the American War of Independence (1775-1783), but migration from Britain to the United States continued, while Canada became the main colony for migrants wishing to remain under British rule.

Between 1830 and 1930 over nine million emigrants sailed from the Port of Liverpool bound for a new life in such countries as the United

States, Canada and Australia. Liverpool became the main port of departure in England but several other ports around the British Isles became gateways to the New World for many other migrants. The migrants who departed from British ports were not all British, with many coming from other Northern European countries, but all seeking new opportunities and a better life.

By the middle of the nineteenth century, half a million people had migrated from England to Canada. One of these was John Porter, and another, his brother George. Their youngest brother, Frederick, and two of his children would also leave England and migrate during the 1880s. One of Frederick's daughters preceded her father and siblings with a migration to the United States.

Figure 8.1 Arrival in New York

What was it like for these migrants as they set out to make a new life in a distant land? William Cattermole, an Englishman who had spent four years in Canada and the United States, on his return in 1831 gave lectures at Colchester and Ipswich to encourage the idea of migration. These were then published as *Emigration: the Advantages of Emigration to Canada* (London, England, 1831) offering advice to those considering migration.

> I have been chiefly induced to submit the following pages to the public, with a view of correcting the erroneous idea which I have found prevails in this country, with regard to the climate of one of the most important of the British Colonial possessions. Canada is considered, even by many otherwise well-informed persons, as a country covered with eternal snows, and scarcely fit for the habitation of a civilized being.

A residence of some years in the Upper Province has enabled me to decidedly state, that such is not the fact, and that in point of climate, soil, and capability for an advantageous settlement, it is not exceeded, if equalled by any country in the world; besides which, from its contiguity to England, the voyage is considerably shorter than to any of the British Colonies, very seldom exceeding five or six weeks, and from the great number of vessels going there for cargoes in ballast, passages can be procured at very low rates.

There were three main motives for migration. Some were fleeing from the hardships of poverty and unemployment. These included the 1.25 million Irish who migrated between 1845 and 1851 as a result of the potato famine. Others migrated to escape religious persecution, including many Russian and Polish Jews. Others, suffering neither poverty nor persecution, were attracted by the possibility of a higher standard of living through migration to another country.

DEPARTING FROM LIVERPOOL

By the early nineteenth century Liverpool had become Britain's most important port of departure. Migrants could often spend a few days or even a week or more in a Liverpool lodging house waiting for a ship. In the early nineteenth century lodging houses were often overcrowded and inhospitable. By the middle of that century migrants passing through Liverpool were also subject to harassment and fraud by local confidence tricksters, known as 'runners'. There were also hazards in selecting a ship.

In 1832 Joseph Pickering, an experienced migrant, sent a letter to a friend wishing to board a ship in Liverpool bound for Canada or New York. His advice was as follows:

Emigrants, on arrival at Liverpool, should engage private lodgings for a few days, near the docks, while they look out a proper vessel, according to former directions. Inquire of the time of sailing – the number they intend to carry – what water will be allowed (a gallon per head, per day, should be allowed, but half a gallon will suffice, but not less) what grates for cooking; should be two, besides the one for sailors – choose a fast-sailing vessel; sails and rigging good, and high between decks; berths near the hind hatchway, for fresh air, and the least motion of the vessel; size of the vessel not of so much consequence, but largest generally preferred. Never listen to, or bargain with, any of the owners of runners that are employed by the offices, which are paid a percentage on all the gulls they can catch; and emigrants will be dogged by them in every street. The principles of these offices I am, in justice for a warning, compelled to say I found to be knavery and trickery of various kinds, which are a disgrace to the country, and show negligence in the authorities in suffering such shameful practices. Hardly an emigrant escapes them. They will engage any number for any particular vessel, and then one-half, perhaps, have to wait for other vessels; so that the emigrant's means are often exhausted before he can sail. These agents also keep provisions, &c., to supply passengers, and make exorbitant charges for very inferior articles, and put on them much more in quantity than is necessary.

The advice of Joseph Pickering continues, giving a fuller idea of what was entailed in crossing the North Atlantic by sailing ship. The emigrants would already have packed their personal possessions but now they must provision themselves for a voyage several weeks long.

The best house for supplies I found in Liverpool, where almost everything necessary was to be procured; it is the north corner, at the top of Denison-street, I forget the name. It is a grocery shop and bake-house; the proprietor is a most obliging and honourable man. Emigrants, when they leave home, must have their eyes open, as they will meet with sharpers in every direction, practising on their credulity, offering the best lodgings, provisions, &c. &c.; but let everyone examine for himself.

Sovereigns are the best money to carry out; Spanish dollars ... the next ... A friend of mine, on coming out last season, was persuaded by the money-changers, to purchase doubloons ... the consequence was, he with great difficulty made his money again; while had he brought out sovereigns or dollars, they would have more than paid all his expenses, by the premium...

By my recent experience I find the following a preferable

INVENTORY OF PROVISIONS FOR EACH ADULT:—

10 lbs. best biscuit kept dry.

4 lbs. toasted bread kept dry.

14 lbs. flour.—Flour is better than much biscuit, as pudding and fresh baked cakes can be eaten when the other is not palatable through sickness.

7 lbs. rice, for puddings.

4 lbs. oatmeal, for thick and thin gruel.

7 lbs. sugar and 5 lbs. butter.

4 lbs. raisins and currants (half each).

2 lbs. cheese.

12 lbs. ham.

½ lb. tea, ½ lb. coffee, of best quality, or it cannot be used in sickness, and often then it is disagreeable.

4 lbs. dry fat bacon, to fry pancakes, and with eggs.

3 or 4 lbs. beef, roasted well on shore, to begin with.

2 or 3 lbs. lean beef, chopped fine, with pepper, &c. potted close—a spoonful in boiling water, with bit of onion, &c., makes good broth.

1½ doz. best Dutch herrings.

2 doz. eggs—packed in salt, small ends down.

Boiled milk or cream, put 2 lbs. of loaf sugar into it when half cooled, and then bottle it; if put in boiling, it will curdle it.

Vinegar, &c., &c., as before; porter as before;—for "preserved lemons," it should have been preserves and lemons. Potatoes as before. Everything should be of the best quality; and other things as before. I have not stated price, not thinking it necessary.

Each family should have frying-pan, two tin baking-dishes, tea kettle, large or small pot, and other necessary cooking and eating utensils—if young children, a lantern will be necessary. Some opening medicine ought to be taken, such as aloetic pills, rhubarb, &c.; for fever, nitre, &c. Clothes, beds, and bedding, should be brought with families, but no household furniture, or heavy articles will answer, except a clock. I have thus given all that occurs to my mind, at present, worth noticing; and I remain, Sir,

Yours respectfully,

JOSEPH PICKERING.

P.S.—When in Liverpool last spring, coming out, I saw several farmers, who came down with emigrants, to ship them off on the parish account. Some supplied them liberally, and allowed them 4£, others 3£ per head after landing, which is little enough; others again, hardly allowed them a shilling, which is disgraceful, as on landing they become less or more, according to health or sickness, dependent on charity, and a heavy tax on the inhabitants at Quebec. In New York they will not let them land, if they have not money sufficient to carry them up into the country.

Letters to Canada, it appears, require a period of three months before they reach the parties; but an answer reaches England in six or eight weeks.

Crossing the Atlantic on a sailing ship in the mid-nineteenth century was a risky affair, particularly during the winter months. Westbound voyages usually took four to six weeks, but severe weather could extend this, sometimes by weeks.

Until the early 1860s the majority of emigrants left Britain in wooden-hulled sailing ships, with most migrants choosing to travel in steerage, the cheapest class of accommodation. Steerage usually consisted of very tightly packed bunks secured to the inside walls of the hull, with tables occupying most of the limited remaining internal space. Overcrowding was common and ventilation was poor, with voyages becoming even more unpleasant during storms. Seasickness was an ever-present problem and diseases such as cholera and typhus sometimes turned into epidemics as infection spread throughout crowded ships. In 1855 the Passenger Act was passed by the British Parliament, laying down minimum standards for space and sanitation; travelling conditions improved thereafter.

From the 1860s travelling conditions improved still further as steam-powered vessels replaced sailing ships, considerably reducing the number of days at sea for Atlantic crossings. The steamship companies also started to protect emigrants during their stay in port prior to departure, with representatives assigned to meet them upon their arrival and escort them to lodging houses which were often owned by the steamship companies. By 1870 almost all emigrants to Canada and the

United States travelled by steamship with time spent on the high seas reduced to two weeks or less.

THE *NIAGARA OF NEW YORK*

John Porter, eldest son of the convict, departed from Liverpool on 11 February 1852 on board a clipper ship, *Niagara of New York*. This 730-ton barque (also spelled *bark*, a wooden sailing ship with three masts - with her two forward masts square rigged and her rear mast fore-and-aft rigged) had been built for an American owner but was under the command of an Englishman, Captain Martin Smith. According to *Lloyds List*, a daily newspaper reporting ship movements from all over the world, the *Niagara of New York* was one of five vessels that departed that day from Liverpool all destined for New York. Migration had become big business.

With 328 passengers on board, the *Niagara of New York* took thirty-nine days on this Atlantic crossing; this was about average for barques. On this voyage the passenger survival rate appears to have been normal: only three died. A twenty-two year old Irishman died of heart disease and two infants succumbed to dysentery. Over ninety per cent of the passengers were from Ireland, fleeing the potato famine. Most of the rest were from England, Scotland or Wales.

Figure 8.2 A barque

Martin Smith had replaced the previous Master of this vessel, William H. Russell, in September 1848. Records show that Smith's early career had not been easy. When the *Niagara of New York* departed from Liverpool under his command in December 1848, they encountered a severe storm and ended up in the West Indies, over a thousand miles off course. *Lloyds List* reported on 20 February 1849 that the *Niagara of New York* had arrived at an island in the Caribbean Sea on 15 January 1849 'with the loss of sails and short of provisions'. When the *Niagara* finally reached New York on that voyage, the passenger list revealed that six passengers had not survived.

Lloyds Registry of Ships had been inspecting and surveying ocean-going vessels for over two decades when John Porter set sail for Canada in 1852. However, the *Niagara of New York* was never surveyed, although she entered and left major British ports frequently. It was not until 1865 that the Mercantile Act (an early example of Health and Safety legislation) came into law, and forced all ships to be surveyed at regular intervals.

The 1852 voyage under the captaincy of Martin Smith arrived in New York on 21 March 1852 and the passenger list was lodged with the New York Port Authority the following day. That was the last time that Martin Smith was in command of the *Niagara of New York* and he was fortunate to relinquish command when he did. His successor, Joseph Livermore, sailed into New York harbour on 15 September 1853, and 38 of his 249 passengers did not survive that voyage.

Because the *Niagara of New York* was never surveyed, it has proved difficult to find evidence of when and where she was built but there are abundant records of her arriving in the US ports of New York and New Orleans in the 1840s. This vessel seems to disappear from the records shortly after Captain Livermore's ill-fated 1853 voyage, but steamships were rapidly replacing sail for Atlantic crossings. The *Niagara of New York* was probably broken up or scuttled some time during the 1850s.

All the passengers on board for the 1852 voyage, except one, gave the United States as their destination. The one exception was John Porter whose stated destination was Canada West (now Ontario). Since John had a specific destination in mind before his arrival in New York, it adds to the evidence that he planned to meet someone he already knew.

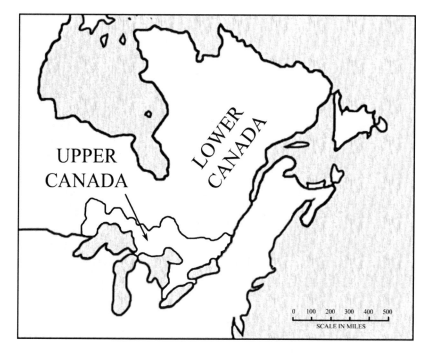

Figure 8.3 Map showing Upper and Lower Canada

ACCESS THROUGH THE ST LAWRENCE RIVER

In 1852, there were two main gateways for European travellers to reach Canada West. One involved sailing to Quebec or Montreal, which are on the St. Lawrence River, then taking land-based transportation to Canada West. Land-based transport meant horse-drawn vehicles because the railroads were yet to be completed.

Over twenty years earlier, proposals were being considered by the governments of both Upper and Lower Canada for building a series of locks on the St Lawrence River so that ocean-going vessels could navigate into the heart of North America via the Great Lakes. In *Emigration: the Advantages of Emigration to Canada*, published in 1831, William Cattermole wrote:

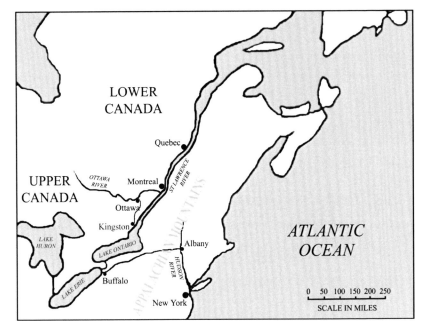

Figure 8.4 Alternate routes to Upper Canada

The improvement of the [St. Lawrence] river is now under the consideration of the Provincial Parliament, and a more important measure for the welfare and prosperity of the Canadas cannot engage their attention. Debarred as Upper Canada is from the benefit of a seaport town or commercial city, by the division of the two provinces [Upper and Lower Canada], the want of an uninterrupted access to the ocean greatly retards the increase in population and wealth, in proportion to her acknowledged natural advantages. A diversity of opinion exists as to the best mode of effecting that object. By some it is contended the Rideau Canal will remedy every inconvenience. Others assert that boat navigation between Prescot and Montreal, from the cheapness of its construction, would be preferable, and answer all the purposes required. By improving the St Lawrence, there will only be 120 miles of artificial navigation containing less than 200 feet of lockage, or in fact a canal of 37½ miles in length will connect Lake

Ontario with the ocean, being considerably less than the Rideau Canal, which is 264 miles long, and has above 500 feet of lockage.

The British Government remained fearful of the rapidly expanding Republic to the south of Canada and therefore supported the building of the Rideau Canal instead of tackling the more obvious choice of improving access to the upper province through the St Lawrence River. The Rideau Canal, opened in 1832, was intended to provide a secure supply route between Montreal and Kingston, which was on Lake Ontario, avoiding the vulnerable St Lawrence route. From a military standpoint, the problem with the St Lawrence was that the international boundary between Canada and the United States ran right down the middle of the river and any improved access to the centre of the continent was bound to be of greater benefit to the United States (see Fig.8.5). In the end, a century and a quarter later, the United States and Canadian Governments undertook the St Lawrence Seaway Project together.

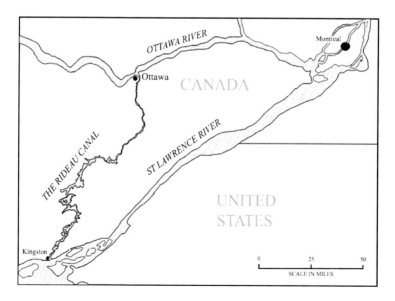

Figure 8.5 Route of Rideau Canal

ACCESS THROUGH THE ERIE CANAL

The other alternative available to Europeans wishing to migrate to Canada West in the mid-nineteenth Century was to sail to New York City, then take a barge up the Hudson River to Albany in New York State, and there transfer to the Erie Canal. The Erie Canal was already operational when Cattermole was recommending improvements to the St Lawrence. That canal links rivers and lakes westward from Albany to Buffalo at the western end of New York State. This allows passengers and cargo to travel from the Atlantic Ocean to the Great Lakes using water-based transport for the entire journey.

Family legend states that John Porter chose to travel to Canada West using the Erie Canal. This was the most sensible alternative and suggests that he had been advised on the best route to take by an earlier migrant. The Port of New York passenger record for John's voyage gives his age, 28, his occupation, labourer, and his destination, Canada West. From this passenger list, it appears that John came unaccompanied by family or friends.

Joseph Pickering's guide to travellers departing from Liverpool also contained advice on how to travel from New York to Canada by way of the Erie Canal. He wrote:

> come by way of New York; as ships bound for that port are less crowded, and the passage is more pleasant. From New York, to take steamboat for Albany: the fare, one dollar each, children half-price. If a number should be going at the same time, three quarters of a dollar each, and sometimes even less; but in such case be sure to have a written agreement. From Albany take a canal line-boat, and choose either the Pilot, Hudson, Washington, or Erie lines, which are the most respectable. If you stop a night or two at Albany, go to Mr Van Horn's grocery-store, about the third door on the pier; but as boats are going every morning, it is unnecessary to stop at all. Along the canal, to Lockport, 266 miles, at one cent each per mile; the passage takes five or six days. They will sometimes ask more, but often take less—however; everyone must look well to themselves in all these matters, from the moment they leave home. Provisions can be had on board these boats, at about nine pence sterling per meal, or eighteen

cents, but families can purchase food anywhere along the canal, and cook it themselves on board, which is more economical. From Lockport by Youngstown, opposite to Niagara, or Lake Ontario, is twenty-one miles; the hire of a waggon for women, children, and luggage, is three dollars. Then cross the Niagara River and the Canada steamboat comes daily to York, passage one dollar each. If two or three families come out together, for a few shillings extra they can generally get a second cabin, partitioned off from the steerage, which is much more comfortable.

Figure 8.6 Route of Erie Canal

CHAPTER 9

MIGRATION EXPERIENCE OF THE PORTER FAMILY

John Porter, the eldest son of the transported convict, must have been dissatisfied with the availability of work in Lincolnshire and would have known that he had virtually no chance of ever owning a farm of his own. He had an adventurous spirit and learned that there might be better opportunities in Canada. He took the brave decision to join the wave of migrants heading off to make a new life there.

THE CHAIN MIGRATION OF THE PORTER FAMILY TO CANADA

When migrants from one place follow others to a new location, the process is called chain migration. The first to arrive send information back home which encourages further migration from the originating location, and the chain begins. Chain migration is particularly apparent in international migration, where it is necessary for prospective migrants to get reliable information about living conditions at their potential destinations. Letters from family and trustworthy friends who have gone before are of great importance. If an early pioneer was unable to write his or her own letters, then others who could write were called upon. Everyone knew the importance of keeping in touch. The members of the Porter family who left Lincolnshire and migrated to Elgin County in Canada provide good examples of chain migration.

Family legend handed down to the author indicated that John Porter came to Canada on his own, which is true, but it came as a surprise to discover recently that his migration to Elgin County involved more members of the family than John alone. An Elgin County marriage record revealed that John's brother George had also come some time before his 1858 wedding. Then records of a death and burial in 1903 led to the discovery that their other brother, Frederick, had also migrated to Canada much later, during the 1880s. Further revelations were still to come.

John Porter's name cropped up as the executor to a Will drawn up in 1876 and filed in Elgin County. The deceased was Mrs Jane Darling of Talbotville in Southwold Township. That Will no longer exists but the Will of Mrs Darling's previous husband, Samuel Pye, survives and it named a beneficiary, Mrs Mary Fisher living in the town of Bourne, Lincolnshire. So who was Jane Darling and why was John Porter named as executor to this Will?

Further investigations soon revealed that Jane had only recently married Thomas Darling, a 74-year old farmer. Both Thomas and Jane had recently lost their previous spouses. Their marriage record named Jane's previous husband, Samuel Pye, and reported her age to be fifty-seven (someone must have been poor at arithmetic because her real age turned out to be sixty-eight). The wedding record also named Jane's parents, John and Charlotte, and gave her place of birth as England. Jane Darling was the aunt of John Porter (1823-1911). So when and how did Aunt Jane get from Lincolnshire to Talbotville in Elgin County?

Jane was the fifth child born to John Porter (1763-1837) and Charlotte Nightingale, and she was still in Lincolnshire in the early 1840s, so would have been fully aware of the problems her eldest brother and his family encountered after his conviction and transportation to New South Wales. Jane had been baptised in 1807, and was married for the first time in 1829 to Henry Shaw, an agricultural labourer. Jane and Henry can be found living in the parish of Quadring in Lincolnshire in the 1841 census, but Henry must have died during the 1840s.

Samuel Pye was born in the Parish of Moulton, Lincolnshire in 1815. He seems to have been overlooked when the 1841 Census was taken, but he was definitely in Lincolnshire in 1843, because he was sentenced to twelve months imprisonment for larceny at the Quarter Sessions in Boston on 17 October 1843. Unlike John Porter, Samuel Pye

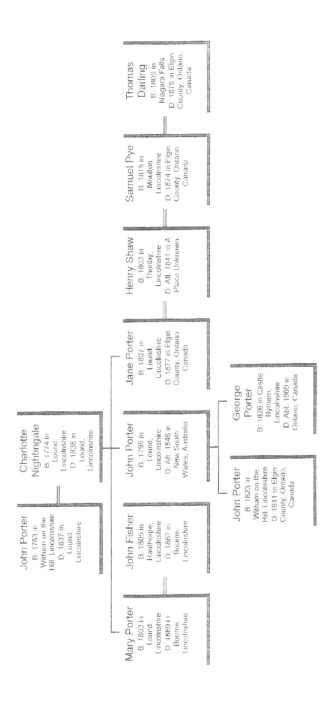

Figure 9.1 This tree illustrates the relationship between the first wave of Porter family migrants from Lincolnshire to Elgin County. Further members of the family came later.

was definitely guilty of his crimes and he admitted it. The value of what he stole was greater than the single sheep John Porter was alleged to have stolen, yet his sentence was much lighter. Both consistency and justice were lacking in nineteenth-century British sentencing policy. Samuel Pye used a false name while committing his crimes and that may account for no record of a marriage between Jane and Samuel Pye nor of their travel to Canada having yet been found. They were, however, definitely living together as man and wife in Elgin County, Canada West, and using their real names by the mid 1850s.

The various UK censuses soon confirmed that Mary Fisher, the beneficiary named in Samuel Pye's Will, was indeed Jane's eldest sister. Mary had led the migration of the siblings to Bourne a couple of miles from their birthplace in Lound but Jane had migrated three and a half thousand miles to a place called Talbotville in Canada with her new partner.

The ship arrival records preserved by the New York Port Authority reveal that John Porter (1823-1911) knew his destination in Canada West when he purchased his passage in Liverpool in 1852. He is likely to have chosen this destination because he knew at least one trusted person who had already migrated to Canada West from South Lincolnshire: Aunt Jane was such a person.

Elgin County land records prove that Samuel and Jane Pye purchased land in the village of Talbotville, a few miles north-west of St Thomas on the Talbot Road in 1857. Until 1853 Talbotville was known by the name of Five Stakes. In 1846 *Smith's Canadian Gazetter* described Five Stakes as 'a small village in the Township of Southwold in Elgin County, 3 miles from St Thomas. It contains about 100 inhabitants; one store, ashery, three taverns, two blacksmiths, one tailor, one waggon maker, one shoe maker.' Five Stakes or Talbotville Royal (to use the full name) is unlikely to have been the Pyes first place of abode in Canada. Most migrants lacked the capital to purchase a farm upon arrival and would therefore seek employment until they had accumulated a sufficient down payment. Samuel and Jane can also be found in both the 1861 Ontario census and in Tremaine's *Elgin County Atlas Map* of 1864 living in Southwold Township. Their fifty-acre farm was located on the south side of the

North Branch of the Talbot Road on Lot 37 (North half of the East half) which is on the outskirts of Talbotville.

When Samuel Pye died in 1874, he was buried in Talbotville cemetery. Jane's final husband, Thomas Darling, died in 1876, having been married to Jane for just one year. Thomas Darling was buried in Sparta, in the Friend's Burial Ground, because he was a Quaker. Jane was a Methodist, but her burial place is not known. The gravestone next to Samuel's is broken off and the piece that contained the monumental inscription is missing, but Talbotville Cemetery is likely to be Jane's final resting place. She died in 1877.

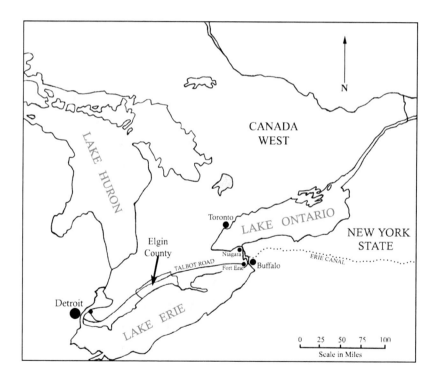

Figure 9.2 Map of Canada West showing location of Elgin County
The Talbot Road was the earliest east-west thoroughfare in this part of Upper Canada

The significance of Aunt Jane to this story, and to the Porter family, is that she was probably the magnet that drew John Porter (1823-1911) from England to Canada. How and when Jane and Samuel came to Canada is not known, but it was probably a year or two before the arrival of her nephew John in 1852.

By the 1880s two railways running east and west and another connecting Port Stanley with London had been constructed through Elgin County and the town of St Thomas had become a major transportation hub. In a few short decades Five Stakes had been transformed from a pioneer settlement to a village with a promising future. But a sad footnote to the story of the Pyes came to light from Jane's final wedding record. The official witnesses present when Jane married Thomas Darling were William and Esther Arnold, a married couple living in Talbotville. William had migrated from England in the 1840s and Esther much earlier with her parents as a young child.

Figure 9.3 Gravestone of Samuel Pye
The wording reads 'In memory of Samuel Pye, died Mar.17, 1874, Ae 59 y'rs. The verse reads
'Hark! Angels whisper me away
My partner dear Adieu;
In the realms of endless day
Our love we will renew.'

The Arnolds were the local postmasters at Iona Station and on a winter's day in 1883 both were killed when a railroad train struck their cutter (horse-drawn sleigh) as they were making their way to Talbotville. Progress came to Talbotville - at a price.

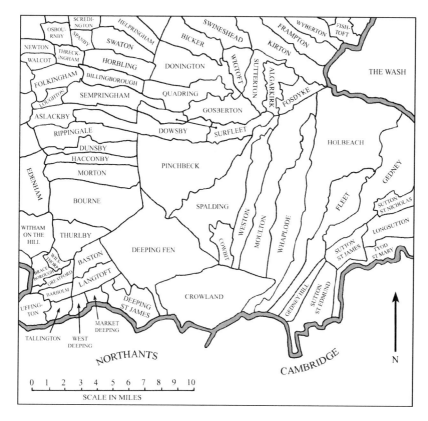

Figure 9.4 Map showing the parishes to the east of Bourne
Quadring and Gosberton are north-east of Bourne

GEORGE PORTER AND HIS MIGRATION

John Porter (1823-1911) had three younger brothers, the oldest of which was George. We known relatively little about his life in Lincolnshire, but assume that it would have been similar to that of his elder brother once their father had been involuntarily forced to migrate to the other side of the world. George was ten years old when his father was convicted and would probably have been able to find some work as a labourer, provided such work was available.

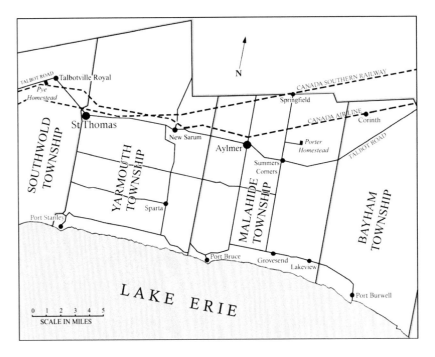

Figure 9.5 Part of Elgin County, Canada West
The Pye Homestead was at Talbotville Royal (west of St Thomas)
and the Porter Homestead was at Summers Corners (east of Aylmer).
During the 1870s two railroads crossing Elgin County were opened.

John must have had some education because we know from various
documents that he could read and write to a limited extent but, given the
family circumstances, George may have had no education at all, and that
could be one of the reasons we know relatively little about him. People
who could read and write tended to generate a greater number of records.
In the 1841 England census, George can be found living in Gosberton,
Lincolnshire, and working as a male servant for William Ashwell, a
butcher. The parents and sisters of Samuel Pye are also living in
Gosberton, while George's Aunt Jane can be found in the adjacent parish
of Quadring, living with her first husband, Henry Shaw (see Fig. 9.4).

Aunt Jane is likely to have provided some substitute parental influence over her young nephews, John and George, during their teenage years and may have had a role to play in finding them employment in Lincolnshire. It therefore comes as less of a surprise that George should also be discovered living in the same place (Talbotville) as his aunt in Canada during the next phase of his life. Since Jane does not appear to have had any children from any of her marriages, there is some likelihood that George was fostered by his Aunt Jane and may have migrated to Canada at the same time.

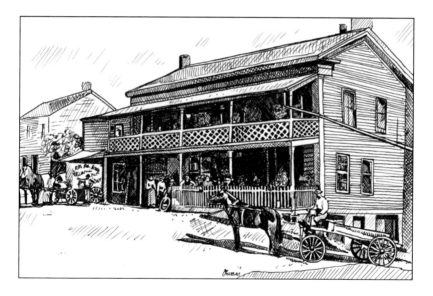

Figure 9.6 The Sparta Hotel
One of several surviving heritage buildings in this village.
John Porter and Rosanna Disher were both residents of Sparta
at the time of their marriage in 1863

Elgin County land records show that the Pyes purchased their land in Southwold Township in 1857. This was already an established farm situated just west of Talbotville and a short distance from the homestead of George Porter's father-in-law, James Bowlby, one of the pioneers of Southwold.

George was married on 18 November 1858 in Southwold Township to Mary Ann Bowlby and he asked his brother John to serve as one of the witnesses to his marriage. The marriage record shows that John was living about ten miles away in Sparta at that time. Aunt Jane and her husband Samuel were residents of Talbotville, where George's wife had been raised. Mary Ann Bowlby already had a son, named Samuel, born there about five years earlier. The Porter brothers and their aunt had come a long way from Lincolnshire but they were all reunited in Talbotville on George's wedding day.

In the book, *Families of Five Stakes* the marriage of George Porter to Mary Ann Bowlby is mentioned but that book goes on to say that Mary Ann returned to Talbotville in the 1860s as a widow.

George would have been in his early 30s when he died but no record of his death or place of burial has been found. Mary Ann did not remarry and died in 1894. She left a Will which bequeathed her estate to her son Samuel, who was by then the foreman of the gas works in St Thomas. Samuel Bowlby never married.

KEEPING IN TOUCH WITH RELATIVES BACK HOME

How and when Samuel Pye and his wife Jane came to reside in Elgin County remains a mystery. We know from census records that Samuel was able to read or write, and that Jane could not, but they remained in touch with their siblings back home, and remembered them through legacies in their Wills. Surrogate Court Records reveal that Samuel Pye left a Will when he died in 1874 which named his brother John Pye, a labourer living in Gosberton, Lincolnshire, and his wife's sister, Mary Fisher, the wife of John Fisher of Bourne in Lincolnshire. The Will decreed that his estate was to be divided equally between these two people once his wife Jane had passed away. Although separated by time and distance, the Porter family bonds remained intact.

Like Jane and the rest of her siblings, Mary Fisher had been born in Lound. From the parish Baptismal records we know that Mary was four years older than Jane and, from their mother Charlotte Porter's death record, that Mary was the informant at her mother's death in Lound in 1838. Mary Fisher had at least nine children, the first five of which were baptised in Lound and the final four in Bourne, indicating that she moved from Lound to Bourne at about the time of her brother's conviction. According to the census records, Mary had some of her younger brothers lodging with her in Bourne from time to time, suggesting that she had become the matriarch of the Porter family following the death of her mother.

So Who Led the Way to Canada?

Since Samuel and Jane Pye were a generation older than their nephew, John Porter, it is likely that they migrated to Canada before he did. We know that John arrived in Canada in 1852 and had a known destination in mind when he set sail so it is more likely that he came to meet someone he already knew. The timing of George's migration is also unknown, but it is probable that he accompanied his aunt when she migrated to Elgin County. Alas, no passenger or immigration records have yet been found which would confirm or deny these suppositions and Samuel Pye's use of false names, for instance, George Smith was his alias during his crimes in 1842-3, means we may never know. What we do know is that John Porter came on his own in 1852, and that some members of the Porter family followed others to Elgin County.

Additional links to the chain migration of the Porter family were added in the 1880s, when Frederick Porter and his children followed and their story can be found in Chapter 11.

CHILD MIGRATION

In February 2010 the British Prime Minister Gordon Brown apologised for Britain's role in sending thousands of its children to former colonies where many ended up in institutions or as labourers on farms. The Child Migrants Programme sent poor children to a 'better life' in Australia, Canada and elsewhere, but some of those sent said they had been physically, emotionally or sexually abused. The scheme Mr Brown was apologising for operated from the 1920s to the 1960s and was reported to have 'ruined the lives of many people'. Brown stated 'I have to apologise on behalf of a policy that was misguided and it happened right up until the 1960s.'

The British Prime Minister went on to say 'It has certainly changed their lives in a way they should never have expected.' Under this sceme, an estimated 150,000 poor youngsters aged between three and fourteen were sent to Commonwealth countries but many ended up being abused in foster homes, state-run orphanages and religious institutions. Children were often told that their parents were dead, while parents were given very little information about where their children were going. Some survivors said that on arrival they were separated from bothers and sisters. In November 2009 the Australian Prime Minister, Kevin Rudd, offered his own apology to the thousands of British migrants who had been abused or neglected in state care in that country.

Child migration schemes were not a twentieth-century invention in Britain. As early as 1618 a few children from Britain were sent to the colony in Virginia, but the numbers involved mushroomed in the late nineteenth century.

Figure 9.7
Anthony Ashley-Cooper,
7th Earl of Shaftesbury

Between 1870 and 1914 Canada was on the receiving end of an estimated 80,000 child migrants from Britain (see A.E. Williams, *Barnardo of Stepney, The Father of Nobody's Children*, 1953). Two towering figures concerned with improving the welfare of British children during the nineteenth century were Lord Shaftesbury (1801-1885) and Thomas Barnardo (1845-1905). Shaftesbury was an aristocrat who set about combatting the injustices he perceived in nineteenth-century Britain. Among his many achievements, he was responsible for ushering through parliament the Coal Mines Act (1842) which finally put a stop to the employment underground of women and children under the age of thirteen. Three times Shaftesbury succeeded with Factory Reform Acts in 1847, 1850 and 1859, but perhaps his greatest achievement was the establishment of the Ragged School Movement.

Figure 9.8
Thomas John Barnardo

The Ragged Schools made basic education ('the 4Rs': reading, writing, arithmetic and religion) available for the first time to children of the very poor. Harold Silver, in *Education as History* (1983) estimates that around 300,000 children received a basic education through London's Ragged Schools alone between the early 1840s and 1881. Shaftesbury did not favour child migration schemes, but after his death many children were sent abroad by the organisation he founded.

Figure 9.9 Classroom at the Ragged School Museum

Figure 9.10 Barnardo Home,
Stepney Causeway, East London

Thomas John Barnardo was a man with a personal mission to rescue children from the streets. He was extremely successful in raising large sums of money for his work which he used to establish care homes and training schemes for children entrusted to his care. A.E. Williams, in *Barnardo of Stepney,* estimates that Dr Barnado rescued 60,000 children from the streets of London. Many of these soon found themselves on ships, bound for far distant lands.

There are two known cases of child migration from Britain to Canada in the Porter family. In both cases, the child migrants married granddaughters of John Porter (1823-1911). One case involved John Lawler, a lad born in 1888 to a road mender and a charwoman living in Marylebone, one of the poorest areas of London. John was taken in by the Shaftesbury Society and placed on one of their training ships, probably moored in the Thames at London. But for reasons now unknown, on 10 February 1905 he was transferred to Barnardo's and one month later dispatched to Canada.

John Lawler was one of 269 Barnardo boys aged between 6 and 19 placed on board the vessel *SS Kensington* which sailed from Liverpool and arrived at Halifax on 10 April 1905. For some reason, this group of boys remained on board for a further day while the *Kensington* sailed on to Portland, in the State of Maine. Perhaps some of the boys were to be assigned to people living in the United States.

John was assigned to a farmer living in Springfield, Ontario, where he was employed for twelve years. He was visited annually by an

Figure 9.11 SS Kensington
One of the ships chartered to transport Barnardo boys to Canada and the USA

inspector and these reports consistently relate that he was happy and doing well. His descendants, however, suggest that he was not as happy or well treated as the inspector's reports indicate. In 1917, John Lawler started to work for John Holtby, a farmer in Corinth, Ontario and that year he married Mr Holtby's niece, Flossie Porter, one of John Porter's granddaughters.

John Lawler was not able to keep in touch with any member of his family back in England. The records of his time with the Shaftesbury Society no longer exist, and the Barnardo records do not include his admission details. John's marriage records reveal that he did not even know the names of his parents which probably indicates that he was very young when he first entered Shaftesbury Society care.

The second child migrant case involved

Figure 9.12 John Lawler
This photograph was taken in February 1905, when he was being transferred from the Shaftesbury Society to a Barnardo's Home

Henry Ward, a boy born in Islington, London in 1878. He was admitted to a Barnardo's Home at the age of ten when his mother had been left in a destitute state after the suicide of her second husband. Henry was the youngest of four children from his mother's first marriage. His mother had two more children during her second marriage but only Henry was taken into care. His two elder brothers were old enough to support themselves, and his mother felt she could secure domestic employment for his older sister, while bringing in enough from her meagre earnings as a charwoman to support his half-brother and half-sister who were then aged seven and five respectively.

Henry Ward came to Canada in 1893 and was assigned to Joseph Jackson, a Bayham Township farmer. He was able to keep in touch with his family and succeeded in returning once to his native England to visit his mother. However, he did not stay long and soon returned to the Jackson farm in Canada. Henry must have been happy living with the Jacksons because he chose to remain with them well into his adult years. He married Ida May Roloson in 1907, the oldest granddaughter of John Porter.

Although there are many stories of abuse and the ill-treatment of child migrants from Britain; the experiences of John Lawler and Henry Ward give mixed messages.

CHAPTER 10

JOHN PORTER (1823-1911) AND HIS FAMILY

John Porter (1823-1911) was an ordinary young person thrust into the role of breadwinner for his family just before his thirteenth birthday. How he, his mother and brothers managed to survive we do not know. After his mother's remarriage, John decided to emigrate to Canada.

John Porter (1823-1911) was christened in St Andrew's Parish Church, Witham on the Hill on 14 September 1823 by the Revd William Tennant. He was the first child born to John Porter and his wife Ann Thimbleby. Shortly after his christening his parents moved about five miles to the hamlet of Counthorpe, in the Parish of Castle Bytham and this is where John would have lived until he was old enough to find employment.

John's father was convicted of sheep stealing in 1836 and transported to New South Wales in Australia for this crime. John Porter (1823-1911) had just turned thirteen when his father was sentenced and removed from the family for the rest of his life. As the oldest son, John would have needed to substitute as best he could for the absence of the natural breadwinner from then on.

When the 1841 census was taken, John was no longer living at home but can be found working as an agricultural labourer six miles south-east of Bourne at Deeping Fen. Ten years later, when the 1851 census was taken, his age was given as twenty-seven, his place of birth Witham on the Hill, and he was working as an agricultural labourer in Sibsey, Lincolnshire. Sibsey is four miles north of Boston and Boston is twenty-three miles north-east of Bourne. It is highly likely that from a very early age John, like hundreds of thousands of other agricultural labourers, would have been hired from time to time wherever he could find work.

John Porter must have decided to leave England and migrate to Canada some time during 1851. He left England from the Port of Liverpool early in 1852 and arrived in New York City five weeks later. He then travelled from New York to his planned destination in Canada West by way of the Erie Canal to its terminus near Buffalo, New York. The final leg of the journey would have involved crossing the Niagara River into Canada West, then overland a further 140 miles westward to Elgin County. In 1852 this part of Canada was called Canada West, but became the Province of Ontario when Canada became a country in 1867.

Upon arrival in Elgin County, John would have sought work as a labourer but no records have been found showing where he worked or for what wages. We discover from his brother George's marriage record that John was living in the Village of Sparta in Yarmouth Township in 1858 because John is named as one of the witnesses to that wedding.

John Porter's own marriage took place in 1863, when he took Rosanna Disher as his bride on New Year's Day. That marriage took place in Sparta, where both bride and groom were resident at the time. Rosanna was the daughter of Bartholomew Disher and Elizabeth Beemer. Bartholomew's father, William Disher, had been born in Germany, but migrated to New Jersey in the United States in 1750 as a young man. In 1788, he chose to relocate again, this time to Upper Canada (later Canada West and later still Ontario). A possible reason for his later migration was to escape the clutches of the New Jersey law men (but this story must await another book). Rosanna Disher was born 3 May 1837 near Sparta in Yarmouth Township, and was eighty-seven when she died in 1924, having been a widow for thirteen years.

It took John and Rosanna over eleven years from the time of their marriage to be able to purchase their first farm. The name John Porter appears in the Elgin County Land Records as a landowner for the first time on 4 September 1874 when he purchased fifty acres in Malahide Township from Robert Hollingsworth (Lot 97 North Side of Talbot Road). Three years earlier, the 1871 census reveals that John and Rosanne were renting a farm near Summers Corners. This census also shows that they owned one horse, one colt, three cows, nine sheep, and two swine and had produced 300 pounds of butter, thirty pounds of wool and twenty-five yards of homemade cloth and flannel during the previous year.

The Porters were Methodists and active supporters of Trinity Church at Glencolin, which was located less than a mile from the Porter homestead. Some years later, the Revd J.T. White wrote an article, published in the *Aylmer Express*, on 27 April 1947. This gave some history of the church and information on the forty families who were early supporters.

John Porter died on 2 January 1911 and his Death Registration Certificate names his parents as John Porter and Ann Thimbleby and states that he was born in England. His age at death is given as eighty-seven years, three months and fifteen days. The fact that John Porter's father was convicted of a crime will come as a surprise to his descendants. This piece of family history was not part of the family legend handed down and seems to have been left behind in Lincolnshire.

Historical records which relate to the Porter family in Elgin County during the second half of the nineteenth century are not plentiful; there is very little surviving information about John Porter, but what information there is about his personality portrays him as well-respected and likeable.

> We were pleased to see our old friend Mr John Porter in town one day last week, feeling well and looking well. The old gentleman is 84 years of age and came to this country from England 45 years ago, the past 25 of which have been spent in this locality. He landed in this country without a dollar and by steady work and careful management has accumulated enough to keep himself and his aged partner comfortable in their old age and he says that they have had a good time also, as they went along. We hope that they will live to see 100 years, as we have no more respected citizens.
>
> *Aylmer Express,* 16 January 1908, page 1

People seemed to trust John as well as like him. Not only his Aunt Jane but also neighbours, such as John Bowen who died in 1886, asked him to be executor of their Wills. When John died his obituary stated:

> Another of the oldest and most highly esteemed residents of this section passed away on Monday last in the person of Mr John Porter, of the 7th Concession of Malahide, in his 89th year. Deceased was born in England and came to this country 66 years ago, settling first at Simcoe, but a little later moving up to near Sparta, where he resided until he was married, then he moved on Talbot St., about 2 miles east of Aylmer. Over 35 years ago he moved on to the farm where he has since resided, and where he died. The township of Malahide had no better or honourable citizen, neighbour or friend, and everyone respected and loved him.
>
> *Aylmer Express,* 5 January 1911, page 1

The tone of these articles reflects well on the character of the man, although some of the dates are contradictory. For example, the first dates his arrival to 1863, the second to 1845. Neither is correct. Likewise, the reference to Simcoe should probably read Southwold.

But why a case study about a nice respectable old man about whom we do not know much? The answer emerges from John's struggle. With his father's involuntary absence, John's early life in England must have been difficult. He was thrust into the role of principle breadwinner for the family from the time of his thirteenth birthday. In his late twenties he needed to make a brave decision if he was ever to escape the economic dilemma he and hundreds of thousands of other agricultural labourers in England faced in the mid nineteenth century. He was a common man, without power, office or wealth, but he had the courage to migrate. His life improved because he took the courageous decision to migrate and he was successful in making the transition that migration required. The author is proud to be able to call such a man great-grandfather.

DESCENDANTS OF JOHN PORTER AND ROSANNA DISHER

John and Rosanna Porter had eight children all of whom survived to reach adulthood and marry. A photograph taken about 1892 of John and Rosanna and all eight of their children can be seen in Fig. 10.1

Figure 10.1 Back row, *l to r*: John George Porter, Frederick, Mary Jane (Jennie), Charles, Florence; front row, *l to r*: John Porter (1823-1911), Almira, Malou (Lou), Annie and Rosanna

1. Almira Porter was born on 1 October 1863 and died on 16 March 1941. She was married twice, first to William Roloson on 25 December 1881, then to Andrew Bowen on 15 August 1928. William and Almira had four children, two of whom died young. In addition, they adopted a daughter named Cora Beatrice Whitecroft. Their daughter Ida May Roloson married Henry Ward, a child migrant from London, England [see chapter 9]. Almira and William

also had a son named William, who also married, but his wife died shortly after their marriage, leaving no offspring. Almira's first husband William Roloson died in 1921 when he fell from a moving automobile. Almira and William are buried in Staffordville Cemetery. There were no children from Almira's second marriage to Andrew Bowen and he was buried in Dorchester Union Cemetery. A photograph of Almira, her husband William and daughter Ida May, her parents and mother-in-law can be seen in Fig. 10.2.

Figure 10.2 Standing, *l to r*: William Roloson, Almira Porter Roloson, Henry Ward, Ida May Roloson Ward; seated, *l to r*: William Edward Ward, Matilda Legacy (William Roloson's mother), Rosanna Disher Porter, John Porter (1823-1911). Photograph taken in 1910

2. John George Porter was born 18 July 1865 and died on 19 December 1946. He married Inez Crosby on 3 August 1892. Both were born in Aylmer, Ontario but had migrated to Adrian,

Michigan, by 1894. Adrian and Ypsilanti are both south-west of Detroit, where the next cluster of Porter family was beginning to gather (see Fig. 11.2). John George Porter was a contractor and builder and a talented musician; his hobbies included making and repairing violins. They had one son Claude, born in 1895, who never married but was elected Mayor of Adrian, Michigan, serving for eight years and dying while still in office. John George died in 1946, Inez in 1940 and Claude Porter in 1956. All three are buried in Oakwood Cemetery, Adrian.

Figure 10.3 John George Porter and Inez Crosby on their wedding day in 1892

3. Florence May Porter was born on 12 July 1866. She married Samuel Dohorty Smith, an American from Massachusetts, in 1887. They had four children all born in Aylmer, Ontario: Mabel Irene (b.1888), Earl Cecil (b.1892), Hubert Ivor (b.1895) and Helen Marion Smith (b.1907). This family moved later to Windsor, Ontario, where Samuel died in 1950 and Florence, the following year. Three of their four children migrated to Michigan and their children and grandchildren are now widely scattered. Florence and Samuel are buried in Victoria Memorial Park Cemetery, Windsor. A photograph showing Florence May Porter is shown in Fig. 10.4.

Figure 10.4 Florence May Smith (née Porter)

Figure 10.5 The wedding of Hazel Irene Porter to Herman Taylor, 27 June 1923, Lakeview, Ontario. *L to r*: John Lawler, Bessie Lawler, Myrtle Olive Porter, Rosanna Disher Porter, Sarah Edna Taylor, Herman Taylor, Hazel Irene Porter, unknown, Thomas Edward Porter (in front), Robert William Porter, Flossie Porter Lawler, Frederick Porter, Bessie Ann Holtby Porter

4. Frederick Porter was born on 14 December 1868 in Summers Corners. He married Bessie Ann Holtby on 15 April 1896. Bessie's parents were both born on the Yorkshire Moors, but migrated to Oxford County, Ontario, in the early 1870s. Fred and Bessie had six children live to adulthood: Flossie (b.1896), Clarence Augustus (b.1898), Hazel Irene (b.1900), Myrtle Olive (b. 1903), Robert William (b. 1909), and the father of this book's author, Thomas Edward Porter (b.1913). Fred was a Jack-of-all-trades and over the years, they lived in Mount Elgin, Harrietsville, Corinth, Grovesend, Lakeview and Springfield. Fred and Bessie both died in 1856 and were buried in Springfield Cemetery. A photograph of their daughter Hazel's marriage in 1923 can be seen in Fig. 10.5.

5. Mary Jane Porter (Jennie) was born on 24 December 1871. She married a widower, Edward Judson Olds, in 1896 and they had one daughter, Ethel Edna Olds, born later that year. This family lived in Detroit where Edward worked as a fireman on the railroad, but sadly Mary Jane died in 1904. Her body was brought back for burial in the Porter family plot in the Burdick Cemetery near Aylmer. Edward and Ethel Edna Olds subsequently migrated to California some time before 1920.

Figure 10.6 Mary Jane Porter (on left) and her sister, Annie Elizabeth Porter.
Photograph dated 1893

6. Annie Elizabeth Porter was born on 7 January 1873 and married William Duggan in 1901. They had five children: Neva Estella (b.1902), Doris Annie (b.1905), John Alexander (b.1907), Grace Alice (b.1906), and Margaret May Duggan (b.1915). William and Annie lived on a farm close to the Porter farm near Summer's Corners. William died in 1939 and Annie in 1955. Both are buried in the Burdick Cemetery.

Figure 10.7 Back row, *l to r*: Mary Disher Duggan (1835-1919), Grace, Alex, Annie
Porter Duggan, Rosanna Disher Porter (1837-1924); front row, *l to r*: Doris and Neva
Duggan. Mary Disher Duggan was the stepmother of Annie's husband, William
Duggan, and the sister of Annie's mother, Rosanna Disher Porter. The Disher sisters
were born in Elgin County, but their family had migrated to Canada in 1788 from
New Jersey.

7. Charles Porter was born on 9 July 1874 and married Elva Flagg in
    1905. They had one son, Arthur Graham Porter, who was born in
    1914. Charles enlisted in the Canadian Army in March 1916 and
    served in the 168th Battalion (Tillsonburg) which saw action in
    France during World War I. Charles was also named as an Executor
    to the Will of his uncle, Frederick Porter, who died in 1903 (see
    chapter 11). Arthur served with the Canadian forces in Europe in
    World War II.

Figure 10.8 Charles Porter (back row, second from left)
with his battalion in 1916

8. Malou Louise Porter (Lou) was born on 9 February 1876 and
    married a widower, John R. Young, in 1904. No children were born
    to John and Lou but they fostered a son, Gordon, in 1909. Gordon
    was born in Muskoka, Ontario, and was placed with the Youngs as
    a baby. They are reported to have been harsh parents and Gordon
    left home in his mid-teens, eventually settling in Timmins, Ontario,
    where he worked in the gold mines.

    Gordon served with the Queen's Own Rifles in Europe during
    World War II, during which time he met and marred Jessie Lafferty
    in London, England, in early 1943. The photograph (Fig. 10.9) was
    taken in 1960 when Gordon returned to Elgin County to introduce
    his children to their grandparents. John R. Young died in 1962 and
    Lou died in 1970. Both are buried in the Aylmer Cemetery.

Figure 10.9 The family of Malou and John R. Young
Gordon Young, standing rear; Malou and John Young seated; Robert Kenneth
Young, age 6, and twins John Michael Gordon (left) and Helen, age 3

Figure 10.10 Old John Porter
(1823-1911)

CHAPTER 11

FREDERICK PORTER (1833-1903) AND HIS FAMILY

Frederick, the youngest son of John Porter and Ann Thimbleby, had the dubious distinction of being christened by the man who was prosecuting his father at the time. Frederick experienced a considerable amount of hardship during the years he lived in England and, like two of his elder brothers, he too eventually migrated to Elgin County in Canada.

Premature death and hardship plagued Frederick and his family throughout his life. Soon after his birth, his father was convicted and transported to Australia with no chance of return. His mother was left with four young sons. The two elder boys, at ten and thirteen, were expected to bring in a small income. The third son, Charles, died when Frederick was six years old.

Frederick's mother remarried seven years after her husband's conviction and forced exile and those years must have been a struggle. Her new husband was Philip Pell, a farmer living in Counthorpe whose second wife had recently died. Philip Pell still had at least three sons from his first marriage living at home so Frederick was raised from the age of nine in a household with elder stepbrothers. When he was sixteen, the 1851 census reveals that Frederick was working as a labourer in Baston, a village about eight miles from Counthorpe, for a widow who owned threshing machines.

Frederick was married in 1858 to Jane Hodson and together they had seven children, three of whom died in infancy. Jane died in 1875, at the age of thirty-three, and shortly afterwards Frederick moved north with three of his four surviving children. His eldest daughter, Elizabeth, had already migrated to Michigan, USA, some time before 1880, so did not go north with the rest of the family. Although Elizabeth settled less than 160 miles to the west of her Uncle John, she migrated independently to take up employment as a domestic servant.

In the meantime Frederick found employment as an oiler in a cotton mill in Little Marsden, near Nelson, in Lancashire. Industrial and technical innovation in the textile industry had fostered a huge increase in the number of people employed in the large factories built in the north of England. Frederick and his children probably moved to Lancashire as a last resort.

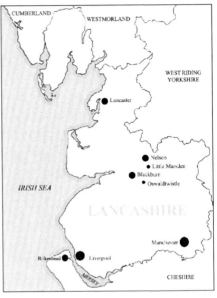

Figure 11.1 Map showing places in Lancashire

The growth of these factories and the rapid expansion of population that came to live near them caused overcrowded living conditions which in turn led to health and social problems. Frederick's three children: Thomas (aged 18), Emily (14), and George (12), were all employed as cotton weavers in the textile industry when the 1881 census was taken. Also in the household in Lancashire when the census was taken was Frederick's new wife, Grace Edge. Grace had been born in Blackburn and was fifteen years younger than Frederick.

Grace gave birth to a son, Herbert, in 1886 but he died at the age of two while living in the workhouse in Blackburn. Something must have gone desperately wrong for this family. If Frederick's obituary is correct, Grace's son Herbert was not Frederick's child, as it appears that Frederick went to Canada in 1884. Grace died of heart disease in 1887, at the age of forty, when she was resident in the same workhouse where Herbert had died. Grace's death certificate states that she was the widow of Frederick Porter, a labourer of Rock Tavern, Oswaldtwistle. Since Frederick was still living, it is possible that she had been deserted. But more likely, Grace was claiming to be a widow simply to gain admission to the hospital in the workhouse for herself and her son.

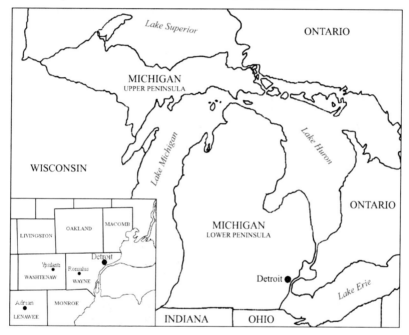

Figure 11.2 Map of Michigan
The inset shows places where the Porter family clustered south-west of Detroit

Some time after the 1881 census, Frederick's younger son George also vanished while still in his teens. He can neither be located in any British, Canadian or American censuses nor can a death or burial record be found. Working conditions in the cotton mills were notoriously dangerous, with long working hours and poor pay. Frederick and his surviving children must have been desperate for a better life. They would have known about their sister Elizabeth who had migrated to the United States in the 1870s and about Frederick's Aunt Jane and his brothers, John and George, who had all migrated to Canada and established better lives for themselves there. By the mid 1880s, Aunt Jane and George were both dead, but Frederick's eldest brother John was still alive and very content in his adopted country.

Frederick's children may have departed for Canada before him, but since no record of Frederick's departure or arrival has been found, we cannot be certain of the exact time of his migration. His son Thomas and daughter Emily migrated in 1883 and Frederick probably followed soon after, as the nineteen years mentioned in the 1903 obituary suggests that he was in Canada by 1884. His obituary reports on the circumstances of his death, but does not completely solve the mystery over the timing of his migration or the situation he left behind in Lancashire. His obituary reads:

On Tuesday night last about 9 o'clock, Mr Frederick Porter, who has been a highly esteemed and respected resident of this section for many years, died very suddenly of apoplexy at the residence of Mr T.W. Benner, on Talbot St., where he has made his home most of the time for the past two years, and with whose father he has lived for seventeen years previous.

Mr Porter, who was in his 71st year, had retired for the night and Miss Benner, hearing him breathing heavily, sent Mr Benner's boy upstairs to see if the old gentleman was all right. He found him unconscious and breathing heavily and called his father, who went to the room, but he was past all human aid and died shortly afterward without regaining consciousness. He had been in his usual health during the day, although subject for some time past to bad spells and unable to do much work. In fact, he was not asked to do anything, but usually preferred being busy at small and easy chores, which he did as he was inclined. He leaves one son, Mr Thomas Porter, of Malahide, and two daughters, Mrs John Gale of Ypsilanti, and Mrs Geo. Loucks of Guelph.

Aylmer Express, 21 May 1903, page 1 column 5

DESCENDANTS OF FREDERICK PORTER AND JANE HODSON

Frederick and Jane Porter had seven children but only three of them survived to adulthood. They were all baptized in the Parish of Castle Bytham.

1. Elizabeth was born in 1858 in Castle Bytham but aged twelve she was a patient in the Stamford and Rutland General Infirmary; the cause of her hospitalisation is not known. She must have been an adventurous girl because she migrated on her own to Michigan in the United States some time before 1880. The census taken that year shows her, aged nineteen, working as a servant in the home of Loring Bigelow in Romulus, Michigan. In 1888 she was married to John Cook Gale, a widower. John Gale was a prosperous farmer resident in Superior, Washtenaw Co., Michigan, with a second home in the town of Ypsilanti, Michigan. Fig. 11.3 contains a drawing of John Gale's farm.

    John and Elizabeth had three children but only one daughter, Eva Mae Gale, born in 1899, survived childhood. Eva married Everett

Figure 11.3 John Gale's farm
This image appeared originally in *Portrait and Biographical Album of Washtenaw County, Michigan: Containing Biographical Sketches of Prominent and Representative Citizens*, Biographical Publishing Co., Chicago, 1891

Stockwell in 1916. They had one child, Gale E. Stockwell, born the following year. Sadly, Eva died two years after her marriage and was buried in the Gale family plot in Highland Cemetery in Ypsilanti.

John Cook Gale died in 1907 and Elizabeth remarried Charles L. Jones, another farmer, in 1908 in Canton, Michigan but no children were born to this couple. Elizabeth died in 1921 and is buried in the Gale family plot in Highland Cemetery, Ypsilanti. A photograph of Elizabeth Porter taken about the time of her first marriage appears at Fig. 11.4.

Figure 11.4 Elizabeth Porter Gale

2. Mary Ann Porter was born in Castle Bytham in 1860 but died in the same place when she was three years old.

3. Thomas Hodson Porter was born in Castle Bytham in 1862 but moved to a cotton mill in Lancashire to work alongside other members of his family while in his teens. He migrated to Canada with his sister Emily on board the vessel *Peruvian* in 1883 and settled near his Uncle John in Malahide Township in Elgin County, continuing the chain migration of the Porter family to Canada.

Thomas married Harriet Hansley in 1888 in Aldborough Township, Elgin County. Harriet had been born in Wrangle, Lincolnshire, and came to Canada with her parents in 1884. Thomas purchased a farm near Dunboyne in Elgin County in 1901, and taught in the Methodist Sunday School. His picture is included in an early photograph of Aylmer High School listing him as one of the staff (see Fig.11.5). Given the family's poor circumstances it is likely that his education began in a Sunday School. Methodists, along with other Christians

(though not those wary of giving power to the people), were keen to teach people to read the Bible and Sunday was the only day most had free for lessons. Sunday Schools soon widened the range of basic education they offered, sometimes with additional evening classes, and once a bright child had mastered reading and writing he had the key to self-improvement.

Thomas died in 1930 and Harriet passed away in 1946. Both are buried in Dunboyne Cemetery. Thomas and Harriet had three children: Emily Elizabeth (b.1888), William Hewit (b.1889) and George Frederick Porter (b.1892). A photograph of Thomas Hodson Porter taken shortly after his arrival in Canada can be seen in Fig. 11.6.

Figure 11.6 Thomas Hodson Porter

4.   Emily Porter was born in Castle Bytham in 1865 and, as she entered her teens, migrated north to work in an industrial mill in Lancashire with her family, then migrated again with her brother Thomas to Canada in 1883 when she was eighteen years old. Emily married George W. Loucks in Ypsilanti, Michigan, in 1887, but they were living in Canada at the time. Arrangements for the marriage were undoubtedly handled by her elder sister, Elizabeth.

Sometime prior to 1910, George and Emily and their three sons migrated from Ontario to Michigan and spent the rest of their lives there. Their sons were all born in Ontario: Vernon, born in 1888 in Dundas; Russell Frederick, in 1891 in Woodstock; and, Roy Nelson Loucks, in 1893 in Guelph.

Figure 11.5 Staff and students of Aylmer High School
Thomas Hodson Porter is at the end of the back row, numbered 4

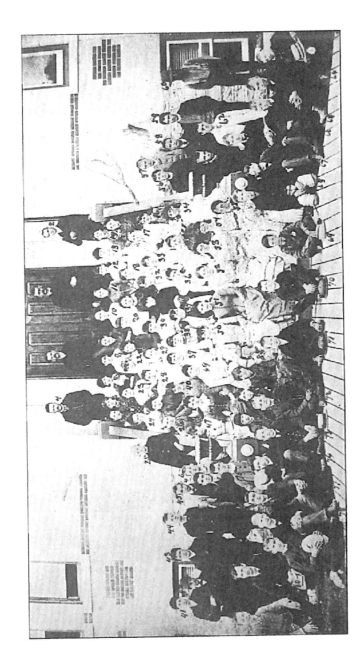

Facing page: **Figure 11.5 Staff and students of Aylmer High School, 1886**

1 W.W. Rutherford, 2 W. Logan, 3 R. Alexander, 4 **Thomas Porter,** 5 Sidney Thacker, 6 Flossie Bingham, 7 Mattie Burgess, 8 Nellie Crawford, 9 Kate Mann 10 Mary Brighty 11 Helen Brighty 12 Florence Marr 13 Jessie Barrett 14 Nellie Moore 15 May Belle Steele 16 Florence Northrup 17 Mary Faulds 18 Daisy DeRenzey 19 Clara Hammond 20 Belle Lees 21 Nina Hopkins 22 Mary Leeson 23 Mabel Wickett 24 Frankie Luton 25 Joe Gundy 26 Nettie Stafford 27 Annie Edison 28 Maud Wickett 29 Nettie Clark 30 Becca McLachlan 31 Winnie Holmes 32 Helen R. Murray 33 Wilmot Elliott 34 Etta McCreadie 35 Kate Barber 36 Ida Jones 37 Hattie McNally 38 Annie McAlpine 39 Cora Brown 40 Sarah Ballah 41 Arthur Alexander 42 Frank White 43 George Hoag 44 Ormiston Luton 45 Arthur Gundry 46 Wallie Hume 47 Grace Miller 48 Jessie Pero 49 E. Hunt 50 ..... McGregor 51 K. Cameron 52 Emma Simpson 53 Lilia Ruckle 54 Ida Cohoon 55 Hattie Hare 56 Henry Kelley 57 Will Clutton 58 Walter Robins 59 William Kilmer 60 Charles Davenport 61 Wilfred McIntosh 62 Frank Closs 63 Clifton Laur 64 Hincks Miller 65 Allan McDonald 66 James Crane 67 Cecil R. Luton 68 George Partlow 69 William D. Scott 70 Alex Sowler 71 Jerry Bosworth 72 John Mann 73 George Poustie 74 Alex DeRenzey 75 John Burgess; 76 E. E. C. Kilmer 77 Harold Barnum 78 Burton LaRue 79 John Dancey 80 Walter Jones 81 Herman Sanderson 82 Jennie Bingham 83 Lulu White 84 Louise Miller 85 Olive Leeson

Source: *St Thomas Journal,* 8 August 1913, page 12, column 2

5. Anne Porter was born in Castle Bytham in 1865 but died there when she was seven months old.

6. George Porter was born in Castle Bytham in 1869 and was still living when the 1881 census in England listed him as a twelve-year-old worker in a cotton mill in Lancashire. No later records of George have been found and his name is not included in his father's obituary (1903) as one of his children who survived him.

Figure 11.7 Thomas, Elizabeth and Emily
Photograph taken about 1920

7.　Annie Constance Porter was born in Castle Bytham in 1873 and died there just after her first birthday.

In 1893, Frederick Porter made the 160-mile trip to the United States to visit his daughter Elizabeth and her husband, John C. Gale. The *Aylmer Express* printed the following snippet upon his return: 'Mr. Fred Porter spent last week in Michigan visiting his daughter. He says this country [meaning Canada] *suits him best yet.*' By then Frederick Porter was a seasoned judge of the good, the not so good and some downright awful places to live. He had experienced them all.

MORE LINKS IN THE CHAIN

Frederick Porter also chose to leave England and migrate to Summers Corners, a tiny hamlet near the Town of Aylmer in Elgin County, where his elder brother John had purchased his farm a decade earlier. Two of Frederick's three children mentioned in his obituary had also migrated to this area in the 1880s. His son, Thomas Hodson Porter, and his daughter Emily arrived in Quebec on board the ship *Peruvian* in May 1883 (see Fig. 11.8). There is no doubt that the actions of the first of this group to leave would have encouraged the others to follow. It is also no surprise that they chose to migrate to the same place that their relatives had selected three decades earlier.

Figure 11.8 *SS Peruvian*
Photograph courtesy of Heritage-Ships

The *SS Peruvian* was built in Greenock, Scotland, in 1863 for the Allan Line to transport emigrants across the Atlantic and operated from 1867 to 1898. This vessel sailed from both Liverpool and Glasgow to the Canadian and north-eastern US ports and had accommodation for a large number of steerage passengers. The Liverpool to Quebec voyage of the *Peruvian* took eleven days to cross the Atlantic, with a stop in Londonderry to collect more passengers. John Porter's voyage, on the

Niagara of New York, thirty-one years earlier had lasted thirty-nine days without stopping.

The ties between the brothers, who would not have been able to enjoy face-to-face contact for more than thirty years, were renewed upon Frederick's arrival in Elgin County. While they were three and a half thousand miles apart, John named his three sons born in Canada, John George, Frederick and Charles, almost certainly in honour of his brothers George, Charles and Frederick.

The younger of the Porter brothers, Frederick, died first, in 1903 and was buried in Burdick Cemetery at Summers Corners, a few miles east of the town of Aylmer, Ontario. In his Will, Frederick named his nephew, Charles Porter, and his daughter, Emily Loucks, as executors, another example of a family coming back together after a long separation.

The elder brother, John, died in 1911. The gravestones of the brothers still stand, just a few feet apart. Their early lives were spent together in Counthorpe, a

Figure 11.9
Gravestone of Frederick Porter

Lincolnshire hamlet, and their lives ended in another hamlet, Summers Corners, in Elgin County, Ontario, Canada. Migration not only takes people away, sometimes it can also tie people together again.

CHAPTER 12

LEAVING LINCOLNSHIRE - IN CHAINS

In 1836, the first member of the Porter family to migrate departed from Lincolnshire in chains. He had been convicted of a minor crime and sentenced to be transported to the other side of the world. His sentence was harsh but this treatment also applied to tens of thousands like him in nineteenth-century Britain. John Porter's sudden departure caused chaos for his immediate family but it also initiated a chain of further family migrations that continued for decades.

Whether the trial of John Porter was fair or just is debatable: certainly the judges and jury were not his peers, they being the educated, the landed, the wealthy and the powerful: Porter had none of these advantages nor anyone to argue his innocence. However, a more obvious injustice relates to the sentence he was given. John Porter and scores of others like him, from the weakest class of British society, were sentenced to be transported to distant penal colonies for the rest of their lives, often for the pettiest of crimes. The practical repercussions to spouse and children for such punishments seem to have been overlooked.

While Britain was transporting criminals abroad in the eighteenth and nineteenth centuries, a few of the most privileged and prominent people in the country were establishing major business ventures in these same colonies. Some of these business ventures required abundant, inexpensive labour to operate, and convict labour was much in demand. The Australian Agricultural Company with its illustrious list of founding shareholders was just one of the British-owned companies established in the penal colony of New South Wales which relied heavily on convict labour.

An earlier solution to the colonial demand for labour had been found in slavery, with huge numbers of Africans taken to the Americas and Caribbean, many of them to work the sugar and tobacco plantations. The abolition of the slave trade in 1807 ended that supply of the cheap labour British business ventures needed in these distant undeveloped places. Was it a coincidence that the judicial system conveniently found a way to satisfy some of the growing commercial demand for the next best thing, convict labour? There were demonstrations and riots throughout pre-Victorian Britain at the widespread unfairness and institutional corruption taking place. Resistance to reform by those in power was robust, and the number of persons transported to penal colonies continued to rise until the middle of the nineteenth century, at which time the practice was finally abandoned.

Yet the demand for cheap labour in the colonies remained strong. Was it a further coincidence that child migration schemes were organised to supply this demand? Fairness and justice appear to have been in short supply during this unfortunate period of British history.

The lack of justice is only one of the reasons people migrate. John Porter's migration was not voluntary, but many people choose to migrate to escape perceived injustices. Religious persecution, indeed persecution of any kind, involves injustice and victims are often forced to relocate to avoid continuing ill treatment. Wars are always dangerous to innocent persons caught in the crossfire: fairness and justice are not concepts that refugees are likely to encounter while fleeing a war zone. Unemployment is a cruel by-product of the economic system that most of the world has adopted, and those that are unable to find work may well believe that unfairness prevails. When justice is absent for long, migration is bound to be one of the options people will choose.

The sudden, permanent absence of the family breadwinner meant that the Porter family had to adapt quickly to their changed circumstances. Two waves of migration followed: one immediate and one which spanned several decades. First, during the late 1830s, the absent John Porter's siblings left the rural enclave the family had inhabited for generations and migrated to Bourne, the nearest market town. The significance of this move, just two miles, but from a hamlet of 60 to a town of 2,500 people, was monumental. At last, they realised that their purely agricultural rural existence had ended, destroyed by revolutions in agriculture and industry and the cold hard fact that the owners of the land no longer wanted their labour.

Second, the exile of John Porter meant his young sons had to make their own way in the world. One died young, but initially the other three did the only thing they could: attempt to find local employment as labourers. We know they were able to find employment, although making a decent living would not have been easy for a boy of thirteen and his younger brothers. As they reached adulthood, they must have begun to realise that their future probably lay outside Lincolnshire with its heavy reliance on agriculture. Lacking control of land of their own they would never be able to avoid the periodic unemployment that most agricultural labourers suffer.

The availability of land in Canada at affordable prices was widely known in mid nineteenth-century Britain and members of the Porter family that chose to follow each other to that country are part of a long tradition of people seeking fresh land far away, where there was a chance of making good, if they proved adaptable farmers. In so doing they were able to break away from being merely agricultural labourers and become farmers themselves, doing the work they understood but reaping the rewards, as well as running the risks, themselves. Migration to find fresh land to farm goes back to the beginning of the human story and is what John Porter eventually achieved by migrating to Canada.

Three of the convict's sons followed one another to the same place in Canada over a period of four decades, each with the same goal: to acquire land of their own. John was the only one who managed to realise that goal. George died young and Frederick's disastrous earlier migration to Lancashire meant that he was too old but his son Thomas did acquire his own farm and made a success of it.

Some of the people mentioned in this book were able to choose freely for themselves where and when to migrate, in particular, the descendants of John (1823-1911) and Frederick Porter (1833-1903). By the end of the nineteenth century migration had become a viable option for people who simply wanted to broaden their horizons. Railroads had revolutionized land-based transport, making migration faster and easier. For example, several in the later generations of the Porters decided to migrate from Canada to the United States. Their moves were much simpler than those of their father or grandfather because railroads had been built between Buffalo in New York State and Detroit in the State of Michigan, taking the shortest route possible, through Ontario, Canada (See Fig. 9.2). During the 1870s, two such railroads began to operate through Elgin County (See Fig. 9.5) and some members of the Porter family gained employment on them. With such good transportation links, frequent family visits took place between relatives who had settled in Canada and the later generations who had been attracted from Canada to Michigan.

Marine travel had also improved. Transatlantic crossings that took six weeks in mid century were taking ten days or less by the end of the nineteenth century, thanks to the power of steam. Travel was fast becoming less risky and a return visit, should this become necessary, to one's place of origin had become a reality. Although none of the Porter migrants ever returned to Lincolnshire, others did. Better information, mainly through newspapers, was progressively becoming available on living and employment conditions at potential destinations. Improved education meant more people could understand the risks that migration might pose and people were better able to increase their mobility as a result.

The majority of people living in modern western countries recognize the need to migrate at different times to find work, or to improve their employment opportunities. For them, fairness and justice are important but not necessarily the most critical issue. They believe that the labour force must be mobile to maintain the rising living standards that many now seek. But fairness and justice remain real issues for many. People should be aware that even well-intended migration schemes can go wrong. Some British child-migration programmes proved to be destructive for both children and their parents, well into the twentieth century. Although these particular ill-thought-out practices have now ended and high-level apologies been given, far too much forced and involuntary migration continues. People in several parts of the world are still being trafficked, against their will, for commercial exploitation. It seems that injustice and migration are still linked all too often.

If the Porter brothers could today be asked if they were happy with their choice of Canada as a destination, the two that survived to reach old age would no doubt confirm that they had selected wisely. Most of the next generation would say the same about their decisions either to seek out new places of abode or to remain close to their birthplace. The descendants of John and Frederick Porter have mainly moved on and can now be found widely scattered throughout Canada and the United States. A few, the author included, have even migrated back to Britain. Migration, for both positive and negative reasons has always been a part of the human story, and still is today.

Figure 12.1
Gravestone of John Porter
(1823-1911)

APPENDIX A SUMMARY OF SOME OF DR BELL'S CASE NOTES

Name	Nature of Disease	Put on the Sick List	Discharged on Duty	Sent to the Hospital	Died on Board	Case Number
Thomas Johnson (Exchanged for healthy convict before sailing)	Pneumonia	12 Dec. 1836		16 Dec. Chatham		1.
Mary Harp	Phthisis	6 Dec. 1836			2 Apr.	2.
Edwin Hughes	Typhus	12 Feb. 1837			8 Mar.	5.
George Wills (Ship's Boatswain)	Typhus	3 Mar. 1837	20 Mar.			6.
Thomas Hunter	Fever	6 Apr. 1837			19 Apr.	10.
Joseph Augur	Scorbutus	9 Feb. 1837			26 Mar.	4.
Thomas Griffiths	Scorbutus	1 Mar. 1837			11 Apr.	7.
John Riley	Scorbutus	20 Mar. 1837			27 Apr.	9.
George Willet	Scorbutus	27 Jan. 1837		Sydney		3.
John Beck	Diarrhoea	3 Mar. 1837			15 Apr.	8.

APPENDIX B

Daily Sick Book of the Prince George Convict Ship

From 5 December 1836 until 13 May 1837
Convicts, showing number of visits to doctor

1 Acton, William x2	33 Butterworth, William x2	66 Franklin, Richard
2 Allen, John x2	34 Callaghan, George x4	67 Freeman, Samuel x2
3 Allsworth, Thomas x2	35 Capper, Thomas x3	68 Gascoighne, William x3
4 Ames, William x2	36 Carter, Joseph x2	69 Gayner, John x3
5 Anderson, Michael x2	37 Cawser, Frederick	70 Gibson, Joseph x4
6 Antcliff, George x4	38 Chaney, Charles x2	71 Gilligan, John x3
7 Applegarth, Richard	39 Charters, James x2	72 Glover, Andrew x4
8 Attwood, Thomas x5	40 Cheesworth, Joseph x2	73 Goodwin, James x5
9 Augur, Joseph x2	41 Cobb, William x3	74 Griffin, William
10 Baker, David x5	42 Cooke, George x3	75 Griffiths, Thomas x3
11 Baldwick, Maidons x3	43 Cooke, Robert x2	76 Hall, Goodwin x2
12 Banham, Robert	44 Corbett, Richard x4	77 Hand, William x2
13 Banham, William x5	45 Corner, John x6	78 Harris, James
14 Barker, John x4	46 Cornwall, Joseph x2	79 Harris, Robert
15 Barr, Robert x5	47 Coulson, William	80 Harrison, John
16 Barrett, John	48 Cross, Joseph	81 Harrod, Peter x2
17 Beard, David x4	49 Croston, Edward x7	82 Hart, Henry x2
18 Beck, John x3	50 Crowe, John x6	83 Hart, James
19 Bedford, Hiram x2	51 Crutchley, George x3	84 Harwood, Thomas
20 Bent, Christopher	52 Cubitt, George x2	85 Hatch, James x2
21 Bent, John x2	53 Darke, John x2	86 Hayman, James x4
22 Black, Edward x3	54 David, Thomas x7	87 Henson, Thomas
23 Boardman, Matthew	55 Davis, William x4	88 Herwood, Thomas x4
24 Bowles, John x4	56 Day, Thomas x3	89 Hides, William
25 Brandreth, Hy x5	57 Dexter, William x4	90 Higgins, John
26 Brandreth, Joseph x4	58 Drew, Samuel x2	91 Hirst, John x3
27 Briggs, John x2	59 Duke, Samuel x4	92 Hirst, Joseph
28 Brims, William x4	60 East, George x3	93 Hobson, Henry x4
29 Burchell, Thomas	61 Edhouse, William x4	94 Holland, Henry x3
30 Burgess, Michael x5	62 Evison, James	95 Hudson, Joseph
31 Burton, Thomas x3	63 Fenbury, Timothy	96 Hudson, Richard
32 Butler, William	64 Fleming, Robert	97 Hughes, Edwin
	65 Flower, James	98 Hull, James x3
		99 Hunter, Thomas x3

100 Husslebee, Obadiah x2	138 Pawsey, Thomas x3	175 Taylor, John x3
101 Hydes, William x2	139 Peake, James x4	176 Thomas, Charles
102 Jamieson, James	140 Pearson, James	177 Thomas, David
103 Jepson, Joseph x3	141 Percival, John	178 Thomas, Henry x3
104 Johnson, Thomas	142 Pettit, William x4	179 Thompson, William x5
105 Jones, John x4	143 Pickett, Joseph x5	180 Thornton, William x4
106 Jones, Samuel x2	144 Pier, Martin	181 Turner, Abraham x2
107 Jordan, Henry	145 Porter, John x3	182 Tylor, John x4
108 Jowers, Thomas x6	146 Powell, William x2	183 Vickers, Joseph
109 Keels, Thomas x2	147 Pugh, Robert x3	184 Wall, Edwin x4
110 Kidman, William x2	148 Purdie, Alex x2	185 Walsh, Thomas x2
111 Lane, Thomas x4	149 Pye, Thomas	186 Walters, John x4
112 Lawson, William x2	150 Riley, John	187 Ward, William
113 Lee, Edward x2	151 Roberts, John x3	188 Ware, James
114 Leese, Thomas x2	152 Rooney, Michael x3	189 Watson, George x3
115 Lingard, Joseph x3	153 Roots, William X 3	190 Watson, Thomas x3
116 Long, Thomas	154 Rose, John	191 Waycott, William x2
117 Lucas, Charles x2	155 Satchwell, James x2	192 Wheatley, William x3
118 Lyons, John	156 Senior, Benjamin x6	193 Wild, William x2
119 MacKay, John x2	157 Sexton, Burroughs	194 Wilding, John
120 Malone, Charles	158 Sexton, John x3	195 Willets, George
121 Marshall, Jeremiah x5	159 Sexton, Robert	196 Williams, John x5
122 Martin, James x2	160 Shackelton, John	197 Wilmore, William x2
123 McDonnough, John x4	161 Simpson, John	198 Wilson, John (age 20) x6
124 McGrath, Edward x5	162 Simpson, Robert x2	199 Wilson, John (age 19) x2
125 McInlay, John x3	163 Skinner, Joseph x3	200 Wilson, William x4
126 McIntosh, Peter	164 Skinner, William x2	201 Wolstenholme, James
127 Mitchell, Richard x3	165 Smith, Joseph x6	202 Wootten, David
128 Moran, Neil x2	166 Smith, Thomas x3	203 Wootten, Thomas
129 Murphy, John x4	167 Snell, George x2	204 Wright, James x2
130 Nelson, Edward x3	168 Spinks, George x2	
131 Nelson, John x3	169 Spratt, Charles	(The records also give the reason for each visit and the dates of admission and discharge)
132 Newton, John x2	170 Staveren, Henry	
133 Norman, Isaac	171 Stokes, William x5	
134 Oakley, May x2	172 Stoner, John	
135 Odell, Abraham x2	173 Sullivan, Edward x3	
136 Owens, William	174 Tanner, William x4	
137 Parkinson, Thomas		

Guards and Others recorded in Dr Bell's Daily Sick Book

1   Baxter, Benjamin (Lieut. 80th Reg't)
2   Buckingham, Edward, (Private 80th Reg't) x2
3   Cooke, Henry (Private 80th Reg't) x2
4   Davenport, Eleanor (wife of soldier)
5   Davenport, Thomas (80th Reg't)
6   Fisher, George (Private 80th Reg't) x3
7   Ford, John (80th Reg't)
8   Frame, George (Private 80th Reg't)
9   Goodall, Ann (wife of soldier)
10 Goodall, William (soldier's child)
11 Harp, Mary (wife of soldier)
12 Haverson, Henry (80th Reg't), did not sail, exchanged for James Faulkner
13 Hewitt, George (Corporal 80th Reg't) x3
14 Hewitt, Thomas (80th Reg't)
15 Homerod, Henry (80th Reg't) x2
16 Leeson, George (80th Reg't)
17 Leeson, John (80th Reg't)
18 Lockett, Ellen (wife of soldier)
19 Miller, Henry (80th Reg't) x2
20 Miller, James (80th Reg't)
21 Perry, Zachariah (80th Reg't)
22 Pritchard, John (Private 80th Reg't) x2
23 Singleton, Ellen (soldier's daughter)
24 Smith, Joseph (80th Reg't)
25 Smythe, John (80th Reg't)
26 Thomas, Henry (80th Reg't)
27 Walwyn, James (80th Reg't)
28 Wills, George (ship's boatswain)

There were twenty-nine rank and file under the command of Lieut Baxter and Ensign Foster, so eight did not require medical attention on the voyage.

APPENDIX C

DR BELL'S CASE NOTES
(This is a continuation of the report given in part in Chapter 5)

A disordered state of the bowels was corrected by stoping the medicine for a few days, the administration of Castor Oil in mint water, afterwards giving astringents: The Mixture: Creta: Tinct's of Catechu *[Areca or Betelnut]* and opium, with aromatic confections, or the Species, pro Confect Opii, I found the most useful. Occasionally in Diarrhoa, minute doses of the Sulphas Cupri *[copper sulphate is a strong irritant, used as an emetic although highly toxic if retained in the body]* with the Extract of opium was given but in many it proved too harsh. *[Note: John Porter went to the ship's hospital with diarrhea, spent 5 days in hospital and was then discharged. The following day he was readmitted with epilepsy, then discharged the following day. He did not suffer from either again]*. Oppression at the Praecordia *[chest]* by Camphor and diffusible stimuli. Difficulty of breathing by Blisters *[hot poultices]*, attention to the clothing, and temperature; and wearing Flannel next the skin. Frictions with stimulating and anodyne embrocations, fomentations, and flannel bandages to the extremities affected with rigidity, tumefaction, weakness or tenderness. Poultices and light dressings, to ulcerated surfaces with properly adjusted Rollers *[long bandages]*, Bathing the petichiae *[scabs]*, and blotches with Vinegar and nitre lotion. Astringent and antiseptic Gargles, occasionally removing portions of fungus from the gums, frequently washing the mouth with warm water were some of the local applications.

In the early part of the voyage several slight cases of Fever, Common Catarrh, Headach[e]s from obstructed bowels, with various eruptions *[rashes]*, Phlegmanous humours *[coughing phlegm]*, with slight attacks of Rheumatism were the prevailing complaints which may be attributed to the change of diet, vicissitudes of the weather and Sea life.

Medicine at this time still focused mainly on ridding the body of bad influences, using emetics like the various compounds of antimony to induce vomiting, laxatives like calomel and the stronger purgatives like castor oil, rhubarb and jalap, along with poultices to draw out infection, and blood-letting. Camphor helped sooth irritations, opiates promoted sleep. They had lime disinfectant, ethyl alcohol as an antiseptic, sulpha drugs as antibacterials. Dr Bell seems to have been well equipped pharmaceutically for the voyage.

By careful attention to the first symptoms, a moderate discharge of blood where the pulse indicated venasection; attention to the state of the bowels, determining to the surface, and clearing the stomach by Antimonials, soon subdued the complaints. - And in the Tropics a diversity of pimples, Boils, furunculi, with deep seated <u>cores</u>, cutaneous efflorescence's excoriations, Prickly-heat, Moon-blindness & Ring Worm. Cleanliness, a correct condition of the alimentary canal, with attention to the various remedies necessary in those cases was attended to.

I regret to mention the death of Hughes, from Typhus. Antimoneal Emetics, clearing the lower part of the alimentary canal by Cathartic Injections, which gives a better chance of purgatives being retained, and causing three, or four, copious motions during the day, Venasection, the Warm bath to determine to the surface, tepid barley water and thin Gruel, as food and drink, in the early stage; with perfect quiet. The dress of the patient and bed cloths were frequently changed, and all excrementitious discharges promptly removed, and by the greatest attention to Cleanliness and Ventilation observed, in the Hospital and throughout the Ship. Hair at first cut close and cold applied. Afterwards the Head shaved, and blistered, frequent small doses of Calomel, and Antimoneal Powder administered to get the system under the influence of that mineral but without effect, during the period of excitement sponging the body with tepid Vinegar and water, and when the heat was much above the natural standard sponging with cold vinegar, seemed to allay the thirst, Restlessness, and induce sleep, also Keeping up an action on the Bowels in proportion to the strength. There was generally some remission of the Fever towards morning, the Patient much less oppressed at that, than at any other period of the day.

With respect to diet, I have always endeavoured to make it as simple as possible, as I think there is no disease the stomach should be less pampered, than in Typhus. Thin Arrowroot and Sago, Barley water and thin Gruel will answer every purpose, without exciting the heart, and arteries. In the 2^d stage, the admission of cool air, frequent change of linen, thin bed coverings, cold subacid and drinks, quietness, guarding against any currents of air, least any pulmonic or abdominal inflammation may supervene. - Calomel, Antimony, Rhubarb, Jalap, and the like with neutral Salts were given in the first, and Second stages, Castor Oil and gentle aperients in the last stage. On the first approach of the stage of Collapse, wine was sparingly administered, and its effects carefully noticed if it diminished the irritation and rendered the skin more moist, and warm, the Tongue softer and cleaner, the breathing lower and the pulse less frequent than before, a perseverance in its use was adopted, On the contrary, Increased irritation, the skin becoming hotter and dryer with a sharpness in the pulse, it was relinquished. After some time, a careful trial was again had recourse to, carefully watching its operation.

As soon as the appearance of convalescence is observed, the diet was light, and nutritious, the farinacea with occasionally Soup, in small proportions, plain simple food given at stated intervals, will best support the strength, and as Heberden says, that fresh air is one of the best cordials in fever, so I think is sleep the 2^d best and every means was adopted to produce both. I do believe that had the boatswain of the Ship George Wills been in hospital during his illness, instead of being in the open air on deck that he would not have recovered.

> William Heberden (1710-1801) was a distinguished physician who recorded clinical observations meticulously throughout a long career, thus making a unique contribution to medical science. His *Commentaries on the History and Cure of Diseases* (1802) was the last important medical treatise to be published in Latin, but with an English version published the same year.

OTHER SURNAMES CONNECTED TO THE PORTER FAMILY

The following Lincolnshire surnames were also connected with the Porter family as ancestor, descendant or through marriage:

Ashling, Burton, Bushby, Denny, Ellet, Faulkner, Harper, Hopkins, Huffer, Lancaster, Medwell, Read, Sisson, Taylor, Warren, Woodward

And some more Canadian and American surnames were linked by marriage to descendants of John Porter (1823-1911) and Frederick Porter (1833-1903):

Birchall, Burbery, Cole, Dodds, Dibert, Dunlop, Eaton, Forsyth, Garvie, Gibbons, Hampton, Hunt, Hurford, Hyndman, London, McCarthy, Partin, Partington, Pearce, Rayson, Redmond, Saul, Schmeltz, Smith, Smithson, Soper, Taylor, Wilson

The present author has some additional information on all these.

BIBLIOGRAPHY

Anderson, Fred, *Crucible of War*, Faber & Faber, London, 2000

Cameron, Wendy and Maude, Mary McDougall, *Assisting Emigration to Upper Canada: The Petworth Project, 1832-1837,* Montreal: McGill-Queen's University Press, 2000

Cameron, Wendy, Haines, Sheila Haines and Maude, Mary McDougall, eds., *English Immigrant Voices: Labourers' Letters from Upper Canada in the 1830s,* Montreal: McGill-Queen's University Press, 2000

Cattermole, William, *Emigration: The Advantages of Emigration to Canada,* London, England, 1831. Published version of lectures given at the Town Hall, Colchester, and Mechanics Institute, Ipswich.

Chadwick, Owen, *The Victorian Church,* 2 vols 1966, 1970; reissued London 1987

Cryer, L.R., *A History of Folkingham with Laughton and Stow Green*, private publication, 1991.

Deane, Phyllis and A. W. Cole, *British Economic Growth 1688-1959* Cambridge, 1962

Foers, Richard, *The History of Castle Bytham,* Castle Bytham Parish Council 1999, updated 2000

Hylson-Smith, Kenneth, *The Churches in England from Elizabeth I to Elizabeth II* , Volume III 1833-1998, London: SCM Press, 1998

Samuel Lewis, *Topographical Dictionary of England* , 1831

Pigot & Co's National and Commercial Directory for 1828-9

Portrait and Biographical Album of Washtenaw County, Michigan: Containing Biographical Sketches of Prominent and Representative Citizens, Biographical Publishing Co., Chicago, 1891.

Post Office Directory 1849

Silver, Harold, *Education as History*, London: Methuen 1983

Smith, William H., *Smith's Canadian Gazetteer*, Toronto, 1846

Thomas, Morley, *The Families of Five Stakes: A History of Talbotville Royal 1811-1851,* Elgin County Branch, Ontario Genealogical Society 1996

Wade, John, *Black Book: Or Corruption Unmasked*, London 1820

White's History, Gazetteer & Directory 1842

Wild, Revd John, *History of Castle Bytham*, 1871

Williams, A.E., *Barnardo of Stepney: The father of nobody's children,* London: George Allen and Unwin 1943, 1953

Witham-on-the-Hill Historical Society, *A Piece of the Puzzle,* 2000

INDEX

(Illustrations denoted by italics. Number followed by f or ff indicates references continue on following page or pages)

See also the lists of names on pages 181-3, and 187.